What the critics say about
THE BEST OF ST. THOMAS AND ST. JOHN,
U.S. VIRGIN ISLANDS
and Ms. Acheson's and Mr. Myers's writing:

"Visitors seeking advice on warmer climes can find it in *The Best of St. Thomas and St. John, U.S. Virgin Islands.*"
—Publisher's Weekly

"A near-guarantee of a great trip."
—Independent Publisher

The authors share their "intimate knowledge of hotels, inns, bars, restaurants, shops and attractions."
—Virgin Islands Weekly Journal

"Essential to getting the most out of any trip."
—Midwest Book Review

"A lighthearted guidebook...full of insider tips and recommendations." *—Essentially America*

"The absolute best guidebook on St. Thomas and St. John."
—Peter Island Morning Sun

"A valid and nifty guide to wonderful places."
—The Naples Daily News

"Travelers to St. Thomas want to invest in *The Best of St. Thomas and St. John, U.S. Virgin Islands.*"
—Orlando Sentinel

Acheson and Myers are two "of our extraordinary writers."
—Fodor's Caribbean

Books by Pamela Acheson

The Best of the British Virgin Islands

Books by Richard B. Myers

Visiting the Virgin Islands with the Kids
Tennis for Humans: A Simple Blueprint for Winning

Books by Pamela Acheson and Richard B. Myers

The Best Romantic Escapes in Florida, Volume One
The Best Romantic Escapes in Florida, Volume Two

"I want to be there, wanna go back down
and lie beside the sea there
with a tin cup for a chalice
fill it up with red wine
and I'm chewin' on a honeysuckle vine."
—*Jimmy Buffett*

THE BEST
OF
ST. THOMAS AND ST. JOHN,
U.S. VIRGIN ISLANDS

Second Edition

PAMELA ACHESON
RICHARD B. MYERS

TWO THOUSAND THREE ASSOCIATES
TTTA

Published by
TWO THOUSAND THREE ASSOCIATES
4180 Saxon Drive, New Smyrna Beach, Florida 32169
Phone: 386.427.7876   Fax: 386.423.7523

Library of Congress Cataloging-in-Publication Data
Acheson, Pamela.
  The best of St. Thomas and St. John, U.S. Virgin Islands / Pamela Acheson,
  Richard B. Myers.
     p.   cm.
  Includes index.
  ISBN 1-892285-03-7
  1. Saint Thomas (V.I.)--Guidebooks. 2. Saint John (V.I.)--Guidebooks
  I. Title
  F2105.A64   1998
  917.297'22--dc21   98-48750
                                                         CIP

Printed in the United States of America

Photo Credits
Front Cover: Jamie Holmes. Trunk Bay, St. John.
Back Cover: Jamie Holmes. Magens Bay, St. Thomas.

ISBN 1-892285-03-7

10 9 8 7 6 5 4 3 2 1

for Aunt Jane
and
in memory of
Jean and Bob
and David

> ### A word from the editor about the authors' research and the timeliness and accuracy of this book:
>
> *The authors have stayed at every lodging choice in this book at least several times. They have eaten in every restaurant in this book many times. They have been to every shop, attraction, museum, etc. They have done all this anonymously.*
>
> *They pay their own way.*
>
> *The authors have also been to many resorts, inns, restaurants, bars, and attractions that they chose not to put in this book.*
>
> *Believe me, the authors have done their homework. And because they have devoted all their efforts to picking the very best and leaving out the rest, they have done your homework for you.*
>
> *No establishment mentioned in this book has paid to be mentioned. No establishment has written or approved its own description.*
>
> *Unlike many travel guides, this book finishes its final fact-checking process only three to four weeks before the book is on the shelves in your local bookstore.*
>
> *The authors' books are the most current books in the industry when they hit the shelves and they are updated regularly.*
>
> *—H.H.*

ACKNOWLEDGEMENTS
Special thanks to Martin Public Relations.

DISCLAIMER
The authors have made every effort to ensure accuracy in this book but bear in mind that, despite what you hear about the peaceful pace of "island time," everything to do with vacationing in the Caribbean—schedules, restaurants, hotels, events, modes of transportation, etc.—can open, relocate, or close with remarkable speed. Neither the authors nor the publisher are responsible for anyone's traveling or vacation experiences.

INTRODUCTION

Altogether there are about 60 islands, islets, and cays in the U.S. Virgin Islands. Most are uninhabited. The four main U.S. Virgin Islands are St. Thomas, little Water Island (just off the south shore of St. Thomas), St. John (two miles east of St. Thomas), and St. Croix, 40 miles to the south.

We love St. Thomas and St. John. Like brothers or sisters, they share similarities and differences. They complement each other, and they stand on their own. Despite their geographical similarities and the fact that they are only two miles apart, in many ways they are two entirely different destinations. Together they offer a mixed U.S. and Caribbean experience.

Although you'll find familiar U.S. staples like traffic jams and Big Macs and large resorts and uniformed park rangers, they're all entwined in an authentic Caribbean setting. You'll also find acres and acres of untouched land, intimate inns, tiny beachfront restaurants, a laid-back style of living, and absolutely spectacular scenery—tropical blue water lapping against classic crescents of white sand, steep green hills, beaches that will steal your heart. It's an "island experience" that is truly unique.

St. John and St. Thomas are U.S. Territories. The language is English (with the delightful island lilt). The currency is U.S. dollars. The flights are frequent. The weather, near perfect.

The two islands are only a 20-minute ferry ride apart and on any day, on either or both of the islands, you can swim or snorkel in the crystal clear Caribbean, enjoy mountaintop views, some amazing jeep rides or hikes, a world-class dinner, and the glimmering lights on the water, over the water, and even under it.

There is truly something for everyone on these islands and it is our hope that *The Best of St. Thomas and St. John, U.S. Virgin Islands* will help anyone visiting these islands have a more hassle-free, enjoyable, and memorable Virgin Island vacation. So set your mind to island time and enjoy the adventure.

—P.A. and R.B.M.

TABLE OF CONTENTS

SPECIAL FEATURES

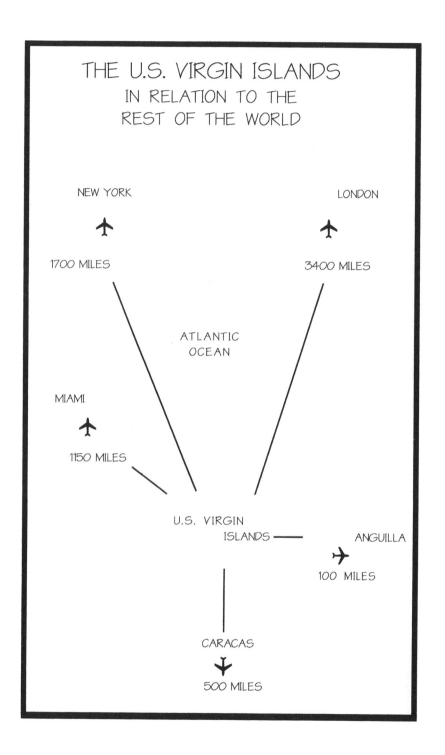

THE U.S. VIRGIN ISLANDS
IN RELATION TO THE
REST OF THE WORLD

NEW YORK

1700 MILES

LONDON

3400 MILES

ATLANTIC
OCEAN

MIAMI

1150 MILES

U.S. VIRGIN
ISLANDS —— ANGUILLA

100 MILES

CARACAS

500 MILES

SECTION I

ST. THOMAS

PLACES TO STAY
RESTAURANTS
BARS
SHOPPING
LUNCH BREAKS
BEACHES
WATERSPORTS
LANDSPORTS
ISLAND ATTRACTIONS

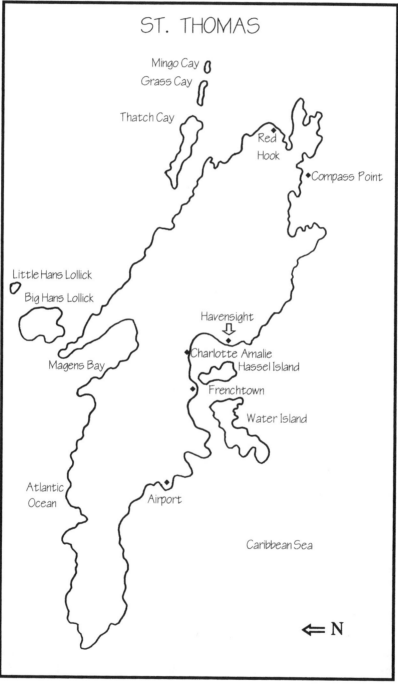

ST. THOMAS

Mingo Cay
Grass Cay
Thatch Cay
Red Hook
Compass Point
Little Hans Lollick
Big Hans Lollick
Havensight
Charlotte Amalie
Hassel Island
Magens Bay
Frenchtown
Water Island
Atlantic Ocean
Airport
Caribbean Sea
⇐ N

ABOUT ST. THOMAS

St. Thomas is a hugely popular destination and decidedly cosmopolitan. It's an island of world-class shopping, fine dining, and full-service resorts but it also has its share of traffic jams, honking horns, and cruise ship crowds. The overall atmosphere is lively and active. Restaurants are full and open late, beaches are busy with volleyball games, taxis are packed with people going somewhere, downtown streets are bustling with shoppers, and groups of snorkelers are checking out the underwater sights. On the other hand, you can easily find a quiet bar or an intimate table for two or a peaceful spot at the end of a beach.

St. Thomas is easy to reach (there's an international airport) and it's an easy place to be. The island offers all the comforts of home, yet it has a true Caribbean soul. It's a great place to go when you want to get away fast to tropical weather, when you want to spend your days at the beach and your nights out and about, when you want to really relax and do nothing, and when you want to be somewhere that is truly Caribbean and somewhat exotic but not totally unfamiliar.

St. Thomas, at 32 square miles, is the largest and most populated U.S. Virgin Island and about 51,000 people live there (whereas only 4,200 people live on the island of St. John, which is two miles to the east). St. Thomas is 13 miles long and its width varies from one to four miles, but this narrowness is deceiving since you almost always have to go up over a steep hill to get to the other side. The island is lushly tropical, rugged, and mountainous and ringed with crescents of white sand. Views from the hills are spectacular.

Most resorts are on the east end of St. Thomas, near Red Hook. Others are near Charlotte Amalie (it's pronounced ah-MAL-yuh). Most restaurants are in Charlotte Amalie, in Frenchtown (which is next to Charlotte Amalie), and out on the east end of the island. Some people think Charlotte Amalie is only for duty-free shoppers, but it also has many one-of-a-kind little shops and even people who hate to shop get smitten. It's also a lovely town. Look for stonework and brick walls, ornate gates and balconies, graceful archways, and colorful doors.

DID YOU KNOW?

❑St. Thomas is on the same geologic shelf as the British Virgin Islands and Puerto Rico. It is thought that several times in the last 60 million years you could probably have walked from one island to another on dry land.

❑St. Thomas is 18 degrees north of the equator.

❑If you headed straight east, you'd cross the British Virgin Islands, the island of Anguilla, and then, 3,000 miles later, the Cape Verde Islands off the coast of North Africa.

❑If you walked along St. Thomas' curvy coastline until you got back to where you started, you would have walked almost 60 miles.

❑The turpentine tree is distinctive-looking, with red-orange bark. It's sometimes called the "tourist tree" because its skin is constantly peeling.

❑The machineel tree can be a real pain. It bears small green apples which are poisonous. Its sap and bark can cause painful blistering that feels just like a bad burn. Don't even stand under the tree in a rain—water dripping from the leaves will burn your skin.

❑The reason there are so many stairs outside in Charlotte Amalie is that the Danes laid out plans for the city back in Denmark and thought the land was flat. When it came time to build, everywhere it was just too steep to put a street, they had to build a stairway instead.

CHAPTER 1

GREAT ST. THOMAS PLACES TO STAY

"There is nothing which has yet been
contrived by man by which so much
happiness is produced as by
a good tavern or inn."

—*Samuel Johnson*

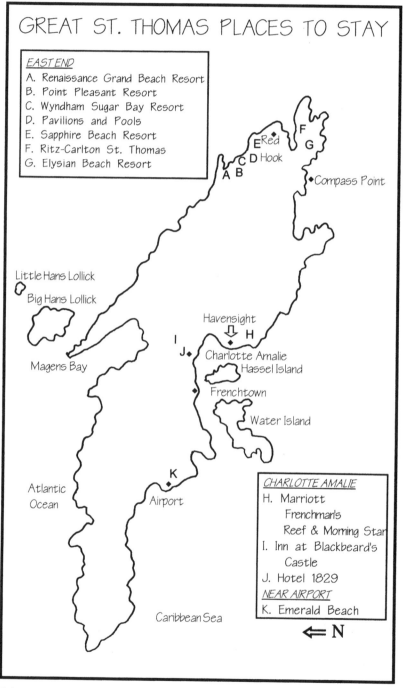

GREAT ST. THOMAS PLACES TO STAY

EAST END
A. Renaissance Grand Beach Resort
B. Point Pleasant Resort
C. Wyndham Sugar Bay Resort
D. Pavilions and Pools
E. Sapphire Beach Resort
F. Ritz-Carlton St. Thomas
G. Elysian Beach Resort

E Red
F
G
C D Hook
A B
• Compass Point

Little Hans Lollick
Big Hans Lollick

Magens Bay

Havensight
⇩ H
I
J •
Charlotte Amalie
Hassel Island

Frenchtown

Water Island

K
Atlantic
Ocean
Airport

CHARLOTTE AMALIE
H. Marriott
Frenchman's
Reef & Morning Star
I. Inn at Blackbeard's
Castle
J. Hotel 1829
NEAR AIRPORT
K. Emerald Beach

Caribbean Sea

⇐ N

GREAT ST. THOMAS PLACES TO STAY

There are all kinds of great places to stay on St. Thomas: full-service resorts that you really never have to leave, intimate inns, motel-style beachfront hotels, condo-style units with full kitchens, and a wide range of rental villas.

Where you decide to stay on St. Thomas can depend on what you like to do. Do you want to roll out of bed onto the beach, or spend the days visiting different beaches or exploring the island? Do you want to avoid shopping, or shop every day, or maybe just once? Do you want a big, full-service hotel with several restaurants right on the property, or do you want a small inn? Or do you want the privacy of a villa?

Generally speaking, places to stay are either near Charlotte Amalie or about 25 minutes away, along the eastern end of the island. There are advantages to both locations. If you are near Charlotte Amalie, you are close to world-class shopping, many excellent restaurants and tourist attractions, and not that far from famous Magens Bay Beach.

If you choose to stay on the east end of St. Thomas, you are more "out in the country." You are not far from a different set of restaurants and close to the little town of Red Hook, which has limited but interesting shopping. Red Hook is where ferries leave frequently for St. John and the British Virgin Islands (less frequent service is also available from downtown Charlotte Amalie). You are also close to the departure point for many charter boat day trips and you are near a number of very good beaches. At most east end resorts, you will also have stunning views of St. John and the British Virgin Islands in the distance.

Rental villas are scattered all over the island and can be found on the beach and high in the hills. Many overlook beautiful Magens Bay.

This chapter first describes places to stay along the east end of St. Thomas, followed by places near or in Charlotte Amalie. Rates are for two people per night without meals on–season. Off-season rates are in parentheses. Rates do not include any service charges or the 8% tax.

17

ELYSIAN BEACH RESORT

What makes this spot special is the combination of excellent service, spacious and contemporary units (many with full kitchens), appealing private grounds, and being perhaps the most central location on the east end of St. Thomas. It's just a mile to the little town of Red Hook and numerous restaurants are within a five-to-ten-minute drive.

Four- and five-story buildings, painted bright white, are clustered tightly together on a steep hillside that sweeps down to a long crescent of beach. The 180 deluxe rooms and suites in this time-share property look out past beautifully manicured grounds to a picturesque harbor and St. James Island in the distance. Units are bright and spacious with comfortable whitewashed rattan furnishings, white tile floors, and pastel print fabrics. The suites have full kitchens and terraces, and some are duplexes with spiral staircases leading to a second-floor bedroom loft and a second private balcony. All rooms have air-conditioning, TVs and VCRs, safes, and irons.

The free-form swimming pool has a waterfall (check out the secret underwater bench behind it) and the beach is a half-moon of glistening white sand. Sailboats, kayaks, pedal boats, beach floats, snorkel gear, and even an introductory scuba lesson are complimentary. Parasailing, dive and snorkel trips, sailing excursions, boat rentals, and sport fishing trips can be arranged. A tennis court, a health and fitness center, and a large boutique round out the plentiful facilities.

The open-air Robert's American Grill is a pleasant stop for dinner. Guests gather around the piano bar Monday, Wednesday, and Saturday evenings to listen to piano music from 7 p.m. to 10 p.m., and the thatched-roof beach bar turns out frozen specialty drinks all day long. Bonnie's by the Sea is a very casual restaurant down on the beach that serves breakfast, lunch, and dinner. Friday evenings, there is often a steel drum band.

You never have to leave the property, but if you feel like venturing outside the Elysian, you'll find that you are in one of the best east end locations. Good restaurants are close by in virtually every direction and the town of Red Hook is practically around the corner.

2 restaurants, 2 bars, pool, tennis court, health club and fitness center, watersports center, shop. 180 units. $169-$199 ($119-$145).Cowpet Bay, 6800 Estate Nazareth, 00802. Res: 800.524.6599. Tel: 340.775.1000. Fax: 340.776.0910. www.equivest.com

PAVILIONS AND POOLS

You'll love this place if you have ever dreamed about being able to fall out of bed into your own very private pool—one that you can swim in by the light of the sun or even the moon. It's not a full-service resort and it doesn't have a beach (although one is a short walk away), but it does have complete indoor and outdoor privacy.

Pavilions and Pools is nestled on the east end of St. Thomas on a hill just above Sapphire Beach. Two long, rather ordinary-looking buildings house rows of delightfully comfortable and very private apartments, each with its own personal swimming pool.

A fenced-in terrace around the pool affords true privacy. All you can see are trees and sky and you are visible to no one, except perhaps a passing bird. You are free to swim or float as naked as you wish, under the noonday sun or gazing up at the midnight stars. These pools are literally right next to both the living room and bedroom area and you can actually step right into the pool from either room, or sit at the edge of the room and dangle your legs in the water.

The units (and pools) come in two sizes. The International features a 20' x 14' pool and 1400 square feet of living space. The Caribbean has a 16' x 18' pool and 1200 square feet of living space. All units have an air-conditioned bedroom, living room, and full kitchen, plus a shower nestled against a sunken garden. The larger units have a dining area and walk-in closets and a bigger shower-garden area. All units have a TV and VCR, safe, and an iron.

This is a wonderful place to completely relax. An informal little brick and stone honor bar is open from 8 a.m. to 9 p.m. Continental breakfast is served here and so is dinner every night but Tuesday and Friday. It's for guests only, and the menu is very limited (one or two entrees are prepared each evening—it might be barbecued ribs or steak or chicken). If you feel like cooking, leave the dishes and don't feel guilty. Doing dirty dishes is included in the housekeeping service (do leave a nice tip if you leave a lot of kitchen messes). There's a video library if you feel like watching a movie. Many restaurants (and an excellent grocery store) are five minutes away and there's a daily shuttle into Charlotte Amalie.

Continental breakfast included in the rate, dinner restaurant with limited menu, private pools. Excellent special packages. 25 units, all with pools. $250-$275 ($180-$195). 6400 Estate Smith Bay Rd., 00802. Res: 800.524.2001. Tel and fax: 340.775.6110. www.pavilionsandpools.com

19

POINT PLEASANT RESORT

This waterfront resort is scattered up the side of a steep hill and nestled in dense greenery. Come here if want a full kitchen and you love great views and like to walk on winding, woodsy trails. The shore is rocky and the beaches miniscule but the pools here are superb and there's a long beach next door.

You'd never know there are 128 units in this resort. One- to four-story, red-roofed buildings are surrounded by trees and discretely tucked here and there in the steep hillside. Great care has been taken not to disturb the environment. Narrow paths (some fairly steep) and wooden walkways lead from building to building, pool to pool, to reception and the restaurants, and off into the woods. An occasional bench or hammock along the walks beckons one to rest.

The apartment-like units have wide expanses of glass that show off the view and many have giant terraces. Generally, the higher up you are, the more spectacular the scenery. You can choose a studio, or one bedroom, or two bedrooms. All are air-conditioned and have full kitchens, TVs, safes (for a fee), and irons. Decor varies, as these are individually owned units, but rooms are generally simply furnished. Those who want the convenience (or pleasure) of a full kitchen, a wide terrace for sunning and stargazing, woodsy paths to hike, and stunning views will find this a very pleasant choice.

The Agave Terrace, one of the east end's most popular seafood restaurants (*see page 38*), sits on the hillside near reception. Fungi's on the Beach is an ultra-casual waterside stop for lunch, snacks, and dinner. Three spectacular pools are at different levels with different views. Amazingly, you can almost always find an empty one—people who stay here seem to be off doing things—and don't be surprised if an iguana wanders by to take a look at you while you are sunning. The watersports center offers complimentary windsurfers, snorkel equipment, kayaks, and little sailboats. There's a small exercise room.

The resort operates daytime shuttles (with fares lower than taxi fares) to Charlotte Amalie and to Red Hook (five minutes away and a good place to get groceries) and evening shuttles to popular restaurants around the island. There's an activities desk and you can easily walk to the Renaissance Grand Beach Resort for a long beach and several more restaurants and bars.

2 restaurants, 2 bars, 3 pools, shop. Special packages. 128 units. $255-$275 ($180-$195). 6600 Smith Bay Rd., 00802. Res: 800.524.2300 or 800.777.1700. Tel: 340.775.7200. Fax: 340.776.5694. www.pointpleasantresort.com

RENAISSANCE GRAND BEACH RESORT

This busy and popular 290-room, full-service resort sweeps down a manicured hillside to a long strip of beach. It specializes in watersports and offers just about every activity you can imagine, above the water and below.

This is the northernmost of the string of resorts that line the east end of St. Thomas. It's set among beautifully manicured lawns bordered by tropical greenery and colorful flowers. Rooms and suites are in a series of two- to four-story grey buildings that stretch up a hill back from the beach. Rooms are spacious with wide balconies and most have great views of the water and of nearby St. John and the British Virgin Islands. Units have air-conditioning, small refrigerators, TVs, safes, and irons.

The beach is a 1,000-foot-long arc of white sand with a complete watersports program: jet skis, windsurfers, pedal boats, and snorkeling. The Chris Sawyer Dive Center and a boutique are at the far end of the beach. The larger of the two swimming pools is just off the beach along with a pool bar and a snack bar. The more quiet, more private pool is hidden away from the beach, across from Smuggler's Steak and Seafood Grill.

There are three restaurants. Smuggler's Steak and Seafood Grill is back among the palm trees and is the place to go for a fancier dinner and also for the popular Sunday brunch and the famous "make-your-own" 12-foot-long Bloody Mary bar. Bay Winds is just off the beach and offers casual dining for breakfast, lunch, and dinner, plus a long bar facing the water. The adjoining Palm Cafe snack bar has light fare and the poolside Palm Bar cranks out tropical drinks.

In the reception building, you'll find a knowledgeable concierge who can assist with everything from baby-sitters to menus of various restaurants. There's also a tiny store selling liquor and snacks (the hotel's answer to mini-bars) and, on the second level, a hair salon, and a W. H. Smith shop which carries superb resortwear (dresses, bathing suits, cover-ups, beach bags) plus magazines, newspapers, T-shirts, and sundries. Service is friendly and prompt, and it's a pleasure to stay here.

3 restaurants, 3 bars, 24-hour room service, 2 pools, beach, 6 tennis courts, fitness center, massage, beauty salon, 2 gift shops. Special packages. 290 units. $329-$389, suites more. ($139-$199). Smith Bay Rd., P.O. Box 8267, 00802. Res: 888.314.3514. Tel: 340.775.1510. Fax: 340.775.2185. www.renaissancehotels.com

21

RITZ-CARLTON, ST. THOMAS

There is no question that this is the most luxurious resort in the U.S. Virgin Islands and one of the best in all of the Caribbean. When you want exceptional comfort and service, superb meals in elegant settings, and stunning views, this is definitely the place to come.

A gracious brick driveway lined with a profusion of brilliantly-colored tropical flowers leads to the formal entrance of this replica of a Venetian palace. It's not until you reach the registration desk, though, that your gaze is drawn to a window and you get your first real look at this magnificent resort—Italian villa-style buildings lead out to a point on the right and, below you, sweeping down to an exquisite pool, is what can only be called "perfect planting." Walkways meander between these beautifully-manicured lawns and blossoming trees.

The rooms are classic Ritz-Carlton, plush and very civilized. Upholstered sofas provide a comfortable seating area. Wide French or sliding doors open onto a very private balcony when you want sunlight and views. Heavy draperies shut out light when you want to sleep. In some rooms the comfortable king-size bed is perfectly positioned so you can lie and look straight out at the view. (A few rooms have two queens.) There are TVs with in-room movies, a safe, iron, coffee maker, and robes. The marble bathrooms are spacious and luxurious for the Caribbean. A separate building houses four floors of Club Floor Suites, with access to the Club Lounge with five daily food presentations.

The air-conditioned Great Bay Grill (*see page 40*), Ritz-Carlton's signature restaurant, is predictably elegant (collared shirt required for men) and serves dinner Wednesday through Saturday plus Sunday brunch. The Cafe serves fine cuisine in a more casual atmosphere and is open for breakfast, lunch, and dinner. For barefoot dining, there are two choices: poolside Iguana's serves lunch and Coconut Cove, the poolside restaurant at the adjacent Ritz-Carlton fractional ownership club, offers lunch and dinner. Each restaurant has a bar and guests also gather in the Living Room to smoke cigars and drink brandy.

The pool is stunning, with a view that looks out over its "disappearing edge" to distant islands. There is a half-mile of beach, three tennis courts, a health club and spa, and shopping shuttles to Charlotte Amalie. Several upscale boutiques sell sportswear and a 53' catamaran goes on daily sails.

4 restaurants, 5 bars, 24-hour room service, 2 pools, 2 beaches, 3 tennis courts, health club, spa, shops. Special packages. 200 units. $369-$499, suites more. ($319-$389). 6900 Great Bay, 00802. Res: 800.241.3333. Tel: 340.775.3333. Fax: 340.775.4444. www.ritzcarlton.com

SAPPHIRE BEACH RESORT AND MARINA

A half-mile crescent of white sand, turquoise waters, and a view of St. John and the British Virgin Islands in the distance provide an exquisite setting for this casual, full-service resort that is popular with families.

Don't worry that the entrance is less than grand. A dirt driveway swings down through somewhat unkempt foliage to an unassuming yellow building and other than the distant view of islands, there isn't much to see. But walk through to the other side and you're bound to like the superb beach and stunning view.

The beach here is exceptionally wide and accommodations are in several tin-roofed, four-story buildings at the far edge of the sand. Units are casually and simply decorated but extremely comfortable. The entrance leads past a bathroom through the bedroom to a living room with a sleeper sofa and seating arrangement, a dining table, and a full kitchen along one wall. A wide balcony that is perfect for lounging day and night looks across the beach to distant islands. All units have TVs, safes, and are air-conditioned.

Tables at the Seagrape, the main restaurant, sit under umbrellas on a terrace overlooking the beach and open to the breezes. Nearby, on the same terrace is a circular beach bar, which is open day and night and which is the site for weekend entertainment. The Steakhouse at the Point is open for dinner on-season. You'll find a casual bar and restaurant out by the pool. Azure (*see description page 38*) is just up the hill and open for lunch and dinner.

The half-mile-long beach curves around the bay in a sweeping arc and is good for walking as well as sunning. Hammocks are strung here and there. While the two ends of the beach are less crowded and it can be possible to find a spot by yourself under a sea grape tree, the center of the beach tends to be busy, particularly at the volleyball court and around the watersports center, which offers complimentary snorkeling, sunfish sailing, and windsurfing. There is a charge for parasailing and renting waverunners. The watersports center can also arrange sport fishing and sailing trips. An on-site full-service PADI dive center offers certification programs and diving trips. Handcrafted stone walls and a glassy waterfall separate the two tiers of the gorgeous pool which is out on a point at the end of the beach. Guest services offers a huge array of activities at the resort—crab races, sand castle contests, tennis clinics—and also around the island, from sunset sails to tours of St. Thomas.

3 restaurants, 2 bars, pool, beach, 4 tennis courts. Special packages. 171 units. $325-$485. ($225-325). P.O. Box 8088, 00801. Res: 800.524.2090. Tel: 340.775.6100. Fax: 340.775.2403. www.usvi.net/hotel/sapphire

WYNDHAM SUGAR BAY RESORT & SPA

This is an absolutely all-inclusive, full-service resort and just about everything really is included. Eat, drink, play tennis, go windsurfing, bring your children in the summer—all at no additional charge.

Staying here is almost like going on a cruise but knowing you don't have to worry about getting seasick. Virtually everything is included in the price of your room: all meals and snacks (and you can eat all day long here), all drinks including wine, champagne, and premium brand liquors (Absolut vodka, Johnny Walker scotch, etc.) during bar hours (which are extensive); use of all non-motorized boats; daily activities; classes; and evening entertainment. Not included are charges for transport to and from the airport and spa treatments.

Rooms are in two tiers of rather imposing three-story buildings that crown a small hill. They are large and comfortably furnished and have private balconies. Some have simply stunning views of nearby islands, others catch the bay, and others look out to the pool and up into the hills. Rooms have air-conditioning, coffee maker, small fridge, safe, and a TV with in-room movies.

From 7 a.m until 11 p.m. there's always food available. The Manor House (reservations necessary and a "Caribbean smart" dress code) serves a buffet breakfast, for dinner switches back and forth from a la carte to themed buffets, and also offers a late night (until 11 p.m.) menu. The casual, poolside Mangrove restaurant offers a different lunch buffet daily and themed dinner buffets. Hot dogs, hamburgers, grilled fish, and other goodies are available at a poolside grill from noon to 5 p.m. You can always find a bar open from 11 a.m. to 1 a.m. Nightly entertainment features live bands, karaoke, and DJs.

It's a steep drop (via stairs or elevator) down to the pool and beach area. A swinging bridge crosses over free-form pools with great waterfalls you can swim under and hide behind. There's a small beach and for no additional charge, you can snorkel, sunfish, windsurf, take out a Hobie Cat or a catamaran, or just lie back and relax. (You can also walk around the rocks, when the water is calm, to the trail to the long Renaissance beach.) Scheduled activities run day and night (power walks, bingo, movies). Castaways is a superb shop in the lobby. If you find time to leave, Red Hook is minutes away. The two-story luxury Spa features just about every treatment imaginable.

2 restaurants, 3 bars, 3 pools with waterfalls, beach, 5 tennis courts, basketball, beach volleyball, fitness center, shop. 300 units. $560-$680 ($500-$550). 6500 Estate Smith Bay, 00802. Res: 800.WYNDHAM (800.996.3426). Tel: 340.777.7100. Fax: 340.777.7200. www.wyndham.com

MARRIOTT FRENCHMAN'S REEF & MORNING STAR

Still sparkling from an extraordinary $52-million renovation, these two sister resorts, Frenchman's Reef and Morning Star, are at the opposite ends of the same property and share the same facilities. Together they form one giant, remarkably complete, full-service resort that you just never, ever have to leave.

Frenchman's Reef and Morning Star are two completely different places to stay. Frenchman's Reef is a huge, eight-story hotel, along with several multi-story wings, perched dramatically on a cliff. Several duty-free shops, fitness center, two swimming pools, and most of the bars and restaurants are also located here. Rooms are spacious and stateside-like and the rooms in the main building are similar, except for the view. Most have excellent ocean views, some look out over the harbor (which is also pretty), and a few get only sky and parking lot. Garden View rooms are larger than Ocean View rooms, but have no balcony. The top level consists of 22 two-story suites. The pool complex, which overlooks the harbor, has cascading waterfalls, fountains, jacuzzis, and a swim-up bar. You'll want to choose Frenchman's Reef if you want to be close to everything and don't mind not being right on the beach.

Morning Star Resort is the place to stay if you want to fall out of your bed right onto the sand. The 96 rooms here are in a series of small three-story buildings that line the beach and are either oceanfront, ocean view, or garden view. Units are decorated in tropical decor and have large terraces or balconies. There are two restaurants and bars close by and a large pool right at the end of the beach. Each resort has its own check-in desk (be sure to tell the taxi driver which resort you are going to), and all rooms have a safe, TV with movies, and coffee maker.

There are two lunch restaurants, four dinner restaurants, and five bars. There are tennis courts, a health spa with state-of-the-art exercise equipment and numerous therapeutic massage and skin care treatments, and a watersports center, and snorkeling, sailing, parasailing, and scuba diving trips can all be arranged. Shoppers can spend time in one of the on-site shops, or catch the ferry that makes daily trips to Charlotte Amalie (*see page 140 for fares, schedules*).

6 restaurants, 5 bars, room service (7 a.m.-11 p.m.), 3 pools, beach, 2 tennis courts, watersports center, health club/spa, 24-hour deli/market. 532 units. $350-$620, suites more ($159-$211). P.O. Box 7100, Charlotte Amalie, 00801. Res: 800.223.6388. Tel: 340.776.8500. Fax: 340.715.6193. www.marriott.vi

HOTEL 1829

People often choose this historic inn because shopping and museums are within easy walking distance.

This National Historic Site is located on the eastern edge of downtown Charlotte Amalie and units vary tremendously in size, furnishings, and price. The fanciest accommodations are in the original building and are high-ceilinged suites with wooden beams, stonework walls, and harbor views. The other units are reached by a narrow maze of outdoor stairways and are plainly furnished. Some look out at the small pool, others look out over the harbor, and some don't really look anywhere. All rooms have air-conditioning and TV. *14 units. $105-$220 ($75-$160). Government Hill, P.O. Box 1567, Charlotte Amalie, 00804. Res: 800.524.2002. Tel: 340.776.1829. Fax: 340.776.4313. www.hotel1829.com*

INN AT BLACKBEARD'S CASTLE

This hilltop inn has a knock-out view of the St. Thomas harbor.

The centerpiece is a National Historic Landmark, a five-story, beautifully crafted stone tower built in 1679 and believed to have been a lookout tower for the infamous pirate, Blackbeard. Some rooms are larger than others but all are comfortable. Decor is eclectic and on the casual side. Although the property is lovely, this hotel is part of a cruise ship tour, and crowds of people arrive several times during the day and wander through the property and use the pools. The elegant restaurant (*see page 35*) is one of the best on the island. *Restaurant, bar, 3 pools. 14 units. P.O. Box 6227, Charlotte Amalie, 00804. $110-200 ($80-$160). Res: 800.344.5771. Tel: 340.776.1234. Fax: 340.776.4321. www.blackbeardscastle.com*

EMERALD BEACH RESORT

This casual, convenient Best Western is across from the airport. It's sort of like a stateside Best Western but with a beautiful pool and beach.

All the rooms here are beachfront and comfortable, and all have safes, small refrigerators, coffee makers, irons, and data ports. There is a watersports center offering windsurfers, sailfish, ocean kayaks, and snorkel gear. There is also a beach bar and an open air restaurant that serves breakfast, lunch, and dinner. *Restaurant, bar, pool, watersports. 90 units. $209-$299 ($149-$189). 8070 Lindbergh Bay, 00802. Res: 800.233.4936. Tel: 340.777.8800. Fax: 340.776.3426. www.emeraldbeach.com*

26

RENTING A ST. THOMAS VILLA OR CONDO

Some people think renting a villa is incredibly expensive, that villas are truly luxurious and only for the "rich and famous." Actually they are available in a wide range of sizes and prices, and many are competitive with resort rates.

Villas are wonderful if you would like the convenience of a house—privacy, ability to walk from one room to another, space, a full kitchen. Some families love them because everyone can "hang out" together around their own private pool (or even in the kitchen, just the way they do at home).

Off-season, special lower rates and packages make even big fancy villas very affordable, especially if several couples share in the cost or you have a large family. Smaller villas can be a romantic way to celebrate an anniversary. One of the advantages to renting a villa on St. Thomas is location. While most resorts are located on the east and south sides of the island, villas are scattered all over. Many are near beautiful Magens Bay and others are high up in the hills, with unbeatable, airplane-like views of neighboring islands.

*One the the best sources for villas is **McLaughlin Anderson Luxury Villas**. 1000 Blackbeard's Hill, 00802. Res: 800.537.6246. Tel: 340.776.0635. Fax: 340.777.4737. www.mclaughlinanderson.com*

Another good choice is Blue Escapes, P.O. Box 8376, Richmond, VA 23226 Tel: 804.497.7024. Fax: 703.997.7090. www.BlueEscapes.com

*Also check the Island Marketplace and Vacation Rental Guide in the back of each issue of **Caribbean Travel & Life**. Buy an issue or call 800.588.1689 for a subscription.*

STUFF PEOPLE USUALLY WISH THEY HAD KNOWN SOONER

CHARLOTTE AMALIE AND A BEACH
If you are staying near downtown Charlotte Amalie or shopping there and also want to spend some time at a beach, an easy and enjoyable way to reach a beach is to catch "The Reefer," the little ferry that runs between the waterfront and Marriott Frenchman's Reef Hotel (which is on Morningstar Beach). The ferry leaves from the downtown waterfront. You can usually find it across from Bumpa's and Down Island Trader. The trip takes about 15 minutes and costs $5. *See page 140 for ferry schedule.*

CHARLOTTE AMALIE HOSPITALITY LOUNGE
When you want an indoor pay phone, a rest room, a place to sit down, or information about hotels or restaurants or attractions or boat trips, head to the Visitors' Hospitality Lounge. You can also leave luggage here for a small fee per bag. It's across the street from the Vendor's Plaza on Tolbad Gade (*see map page 65*). This place is run entirely by volunteers, so please leave a small donation if you can.

ST. JOHN AND THE BRITISH VIRGIN ISLANDS
It is really easy to head over to one of these islands for a day and it can be a great adventure, so build it into your schedule. Each island is different, so choose the one you think you'll like the most or see them all by flying over them on the Seaborne seaplane (*see page 94*) or taking a boat trip (*see page 94-95*). For more specific information, see page 52 for St. Croix, page 94 for the BVI, and page 77 for an evening on St. John (as well as the entire section on St. John, which begins on page 97).

THINGS TO NOTICE
ON
ST. THOMAS

The tourists who didn't pack a carry-on.
They are the ones strolling the beach in their
winter clothes, sleeves rolled up.

The green flash
as the sun settles into the Caribbean.

Shooting stars and satellites—if you gaze at the
night sky for 15 minutes, you'll see at least one.
Guaranteed.

How close the stars look—as if you could just
reach out and touch them.

Phosphorescence lighting up the night sea.

The delightful donkey at Drake's Seat.

Iguanas—they are a little ugly but they know
how to relax.

Beautiful hummingbirds hanging around
the hibiscus blossoms.

MONEY-SAVING HINTS

❑Traveling to and staying in St. Thomas or St. John in the "off season" can save you up to about 40%.

❑No matter what time of the year you are traveling always inquire about any special packages that might be available.

❑In comparing the cost of lodging choices, be sure you are comparing apples to apples. Some room rates might include a continental breakfast or a full breakfast or no breakfast. Know what you are paying for.

❑Ask what meal plans and meal options are available.

❑Also ask what "taxes" and service charges and surcharges will be added to your lodging bill. You don't want a 20% surprise at the end of your stay

❑Calls home to the States from your hotel room may cost substantially more than a nearby pay phone, a special USA Direct line, or even your own cell phone. Check it out before you dial.

❑To avoid any possible problem always agree on the total cost of a taxi ride before you leave and the total cost of a rental or charter before you sign up.

CHAPTER 2

GREAT
ST. THOMAS
RESTAURANTS

"Part of the secret of success in life
is to eat what you like and
let the food fight it out inside."

—*Mark Twain*

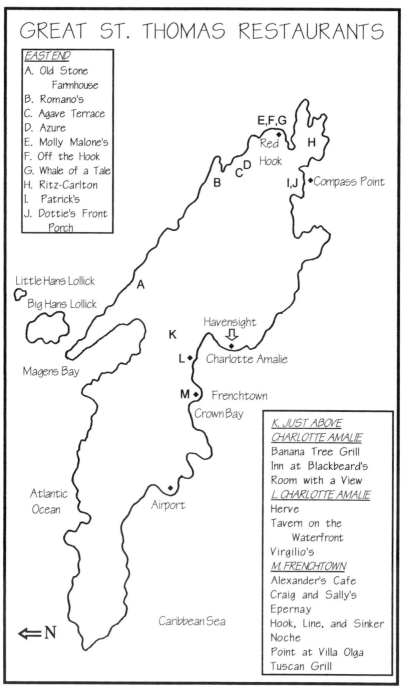

GREAT ST. THOMAS RESTAURANTS

EAST END

A. Old Stone
   Farmhouse
B. Romano's
C. Agave Terrace
D. Azure
E. Molly Malone's
F. Off the Hook
G. Whale of a Tale
H. Ritz-Carlton
I. Patrick's
J. Dottie's Front
   Porch

E,F,G
Red Hook
H
C D
B
I,J ◆ Compass Point

Little Hans Lollick
Big Hans Lollick

A

Havensight
K
⇩
L ◆ Charlotte Amalie
Magens Bay
M ◆ Frenchtown
Crown Bay

**K. JUST ABOVE
CHARLOTTE AMALIE**
Banana Tree Grill
Inn at Blackbeard's
Room with a View
L. CHARLOTTE AMALIE
Herve
Tavern on the
   Waterfront
Virgilio's
M. FRENCHTOWN
Alexander's Cafe
Craig and Sally's
Epernay
Hook, Line, and Sinker
Noche
Point at Villa Olga
Tuscan Grill

Atlantic
Ocean
Airport

Caribbean Sea

⇐N

GREAT ST. THOMAS RESTAURANTS

St. Thomas is a sophisticated island and has many great restaurants. Some are elegant and some are casual. Some are air-conditioned and indoors and some are open to the Caribbean breezes and look out at great nighttime views. There are many highly-skilled chefs on St. Thomas and you can expect to sample some of the best food anywhere. You will find all kinds of cuisine—Italian, German, Continental, Spanish, and West Indian. Local fish to look for on the menu include wahoo, mahi mahi, swordfish, and tuna.

Most restaurants on St. Thomas are either clustered in or above Charlotte Amalie and in Frenchtown (which is on the west side of the St. Thomas Harbor, just a two-minute cab ride from Charlotte Amalie), or they are out on the east end of the island in or near Red Hook. In the evening it's about a 20- to 25-minute ride between the two areas (longer during rush hour). One-way taxi fare is $8 to $9 per person for two or more people. The same taxi that takes you to your restaurant will pick you up also, if you want. Bear in mind that, off-season, hours and days of operation may vary somewhat and it is a good idea to call ahead and check.

DOWNTOWN CHARLOTTE AMALIE RESTAURANTS

HERVE

Dramatic floor-to-ceiling windows capture a stunning view of Charlotte Amalie and the harbor at this delightful hillside restaurant. Relax in air-conditioned comfort and enjoy some of the island's finest cuisine. Although the menu is not traditionally French, it is definitely inspired by the French owners. Tables are well-spaced and elegantly set and this is the place to come for appetizers such as pistachio-crusted brie, warm smoked quail, and escargots. Superb dinner choices include lobster St. Jacques as well as bouillabaisse, black-sesame-crusted tuna, lamb chops stuffed with spinach, and roasted breast of duck. For dessert, try the little chocolate cups brimming with berries or the rich creme caramel. The wine list is excellent and there are many by the glass. Check out the black-and-white photos of St. Thomas back in the gas lamp and horse-and-buggy days. *See page 74 for lunch description. Reservations are a good idea for dinner. No lunch Sun. 340.777.9703. Government Hill. LD $$-$$$*

33

TAVERN ON THE WATERFRONT

This upstairs, air-conditioned restaurant is a welcome retreat from the hustle and bustle below. A cathedral ceiling gives a feeling of space and windows along the front wall look out across the harbor with cruise ships docked in the distance and sailboats bobbing about. An amusing trompe l'oeil painting on one wall looks like a window facing east along Waterfront Highway, but it can't be real because there is absolutely no traffic! Romantics may want to choose one of the two private outdoor tables at each end of the dining room. To start, consider sharing the delicious Mediterranean Sampler, a plate of baba ganoush, hummus, olives, and grilled pita bread; or try the escargots or the brie and bacon. Move on to ahi tuna or grilled mahi mahi or spicy pork ribs. *See page 75 for lunch description. Reservations necessary for dinner. Closed Sun. 340.776.4328. Waterfront Hwy. at Royal Dane Mall. LD $$-$$$*

VIRGILIO'S

Exceptional northern Italian cuisine is served indoors in an elegant, intimate atmosphere. Walk into this dark and cozy air-conditioned restaurant and the rest of the world melts away. Two-story exposed brick walls are hung with a marvelous mix of all sizes of framed paintings and prints. Although tables are quite close together, in most cases, once seated, you forget you have neighbors. The menu offers everything from veal saltimbocca to chicken cacciatore, filet mignon, and capellini with a fresh tomato sauce, plus daily specials. If what you want is not on the menu, do ask. The extensive wine list includes inexpensive wines, but if you feel like splurging you can always order the Biondi-Santi Brunello Reserva 1945 for $2,500. Don't leave without trying a Virgilio's cappuccino. *See page 75 for lunch description. Reservations a must. Closed Sun. 340.776.4920. Stortvaer Gade, between Main and Back St. LD $$-$$$*

RESTAURANTS JUST ABOVE CHARLOTTE AMALIE
BANANA TREE GRILL

Legendary St. Thomas restauranteurs Liz and Jerry Buckalew are the masterminds behind this appealing restaurant perched on a high hill with an absolutely stunning view. Tables are on a broad terrace way above Charlotte Amalie and the harbor and are open to the gentle Caribbean breezes. At twilight time and after dark the scene of the twinkling lights below and in the hills is simply magical. In fact, one of the great sights here is seeing a big full moon come popping out from behind the hills of St. Thomas. Dine on garlic-lime mahi mahi, sesame-seared tuna, filet mignon with gorgonzola cream, or a light vegetable medley over spaghettini. Grilled shrimp or lobster tempura are tasty starter choices and the Godiva chocolate brownies are thrilling. There's a cozy little bar just inside the entrance. *Reservations necessary. Closed Mon. 340.776.4050. Bluebeard's Castle on Bluebeard Hill. D $$-$$$*

INN AT BLACKBEARD'S CASTLE RESTAURANT

This peaceful al fresco choice sits on a hillside overlooking Charlotte Amalie. The view at night is lovely, with the lights of downtown and in the hills shimmering in the distance. Most tables are on a covered terrace but a few are completely out in the open, and these are quite romantic on a starry or moonlit night. The menu is Caribbean-inspired and creative and the results are a delight. Try the baby arugula salad crowned with a warm goat cheese crostini or the Caribbean spiced crab cake or the signature fiesta salad for a starter. Next consider the pan-seared diver scallops with fresh mango salsa or the penne puttanesca or the ahi tuna on couscous with oven-roasted tomatoes, olives, and fresh mint. The well-known and talented chef turns out superb cuisine. Everything is excellent here. *Reservations necessary. Closed Sun. 340.776.1234. Blackbeard's Castle. D $$-$$$*

ROOM WITH A VIEW

The decor is swanky 1940s and the view is stunning at this appealing, air-conditioned wine bar and bistro. A dramatic floor-to-ceiling window at the far end of the room frames a spectacular view of town, the harbor, and the hills beyond. Sunsets here are gorgeous. You can see planes approaching and leaving the airport and at night you can watch the planes' headlights and gaze out at the glittering lights of Charlotte Amalie. The room itself is quite dark, with a little lamp on each table. There's a wine list (by the glass or bottle) and daily wine specials. The crab crepe, French onion soup, and brie almondine make good appetizers. For a main course, try the excellent lasagna, Creole shrimp, chicken marsala, or one of the fresh catches of the day. Ice cream sundaes are a specialty. *Late night menu from 10 p.m. to 1 a.m. Closed Sun. 340.774.2377. Bluebeard's Castle, Bluebeard Hill. D $$*

FRENCHTOWN RESTAURANTS
ALEXANDER'S CAFE

Excellently-prepared German and Austrian cuisine is served side-by-side with grilled fresh fish, pasta, and even Vietnamese dishes at this stylish, sophisticated, air-conditioned stop. The walls are pink, the furnishings are lacquer black, the tablecloths are crisp and white, and the overall effect is striking. This is a very small restaurant with a superb chef, a classy atmosphere, and a remarkably varied menu. You can come here for delicious, authentic weiner schnitzel or jaeger schnitzel (veal in a mushroom cream sauce). You can have pasta with several excellent sauces including a meat sauce, a pesto, and a Cajun concoction. You can also dine on seared ginger tuna or sirloin with brandy and green peppercorn sauce. Various salads and beef carpaccio are delightful beginnings. *Reservations necessary for dinner. Closed Sun. 340.774.4349. Frenchtown Mall. LD $$-$$$*

CRAIG AND SALLY'S

Two owners who really care, a great (albeit extremely eclectic) menu, and excellent food served in a casual but cosmopolitan atmosphere make this place worth coming back to again and again. There are seascape murals on the walls, five or six different air-conditioned dining areas, and comfortable low lighting. Craig and Sally love to run a restaurant and it shows. The inspired and lengthy menu changes nightly and bears thorough investigation. One night the filet mignon might be stuffed with Danish blue cheese; the next night it might be served atop garlic-roasted/smoked mozzarella mashed potatoes. One night you might find Atlantic salmon over spiced-rum mashed sweet potatoes and the next night it might be over baby leaf spinach with a warm vinaigrette sauce. Tuna, sea bass, pasta, lamb, veal, duck—you'll find it all, prepared in wonderful ways. Sooner or later you'll notice that crates of wine are stacked here and there all over the place. Craig is the wine connoisseur and offers ones that are truly unusual. Check and see what he's got when you're there. Some wines are real bargains. There's a large, comfortable bar also. *Reservations necessary. Closed Mon.-Tues. No lunch Sat.-Tues. 340.777.9949. Frenchtown. LD $$-$$$*

EPERNAY

Small tables run along one side of this tiny, dark, and sophisticated wine bar and bistro with a classy decor. Hung from the ceiling are green shades, which hover just above the tables, giving off an intimate glow. The inside is air-conditioned. A few tables are also outside. The menu choices are quite varied. Begin with a warm spinach salad with blue cheese or a classic Caesar, or fried calamari with lemon-mayonnaise remoulade. Entrees include angel hair pommodoro, sesame-crusted tuna with sticky rice and vegetables, marinated rib eye with fried shallots, and a cheese quesadilla with chicken. Or try the sushi menu. Or just have one after another of the tempting appetizers: polenta with mushroom ragout, tuna tartare, grilled eggplant, or the Epernay Platter with smoked salmon, brie, and pate. *Closed Sun., no lunch Sat. Dinner until 11 p.m.; Fri., Sat. until midnight. 340.774.5348. Frenchtown Mall. LD $-$$*

HOOK, LINE, AND SINKER

When you are in the mood for a casual diner/coffee shop atmosphere and menu plus outstanding food, this is the place to come. The building is attractive weathered wood outside, and inside the decor is on the plain side, with booths along the walls, simple tables, and a counter where you can eat. Windows are open to tropical breezes and you can see pelicans diving for food. This is the kind of place that you could come to seven days in a row for breakfast, lunch, and dinner and have something different and it would all be good. Hamburgers (available lunch and dinner) are great but so is the chili and the salads and the lunchtime sandwiches. There's a terrific Reuben and also a great Black Russian (pumpernickel plus corned beef, turkey, and coleslaw). For dinner, choose pasta dishes, or fresh fish such as grilled swordfish or pecan-coated red snapper, or the London broil with homemade mashed potatoes. Check the blackboard for great daily specials like the roast turkey platter or the great Chili Taco Salad. *Open 7 a.m., except Sun. when it's brunch only 10 a.m.-2:30 p.m. 340.776.9708. Frenchtown. BLD $-$$*

NOCHE

Dramatic decor and dim lighting set the scene for a delightful meal at this dark and spacious air-conditioned restaurant. The enticing menu features a mixture of Mexican, Spanish, and South American cuisines. For a festive beginning, try an order of the guacamole, their signature dish, which is prepared tableside. Other good starter choices include corn chips with the Sante Fe salsa or the fontina fondue with olives, chimichurri, and roasted red peppers. For the main course, good bets are the cheesy chicken enchiladas, the beef tenderloin with chipotle cheddar mashed potatoes, and the mesquite grilled salmon with citrus salsa and spanish rice. The lunch menu includes tacos, burgers, chile rellenos, and tostadas. *No lunch Sat., Sun. 340.774.3800. Frenchtown. LD $$*

POINT AT VILLA OLGA

Come here for true al fresco dining overlooking the water. This restaurant is right at the end of a point of land and there are no walls, just a tin roof and a broad terrace and nicely-spaced tables. The view looks out to East Gregorie Channel and Water and Hassel Islands. The menu is basically Continental and features prime rib and grilled steaks, chicken, and fresh local fish. There is also an enormous salad bar which you can have as a full meal if you so desire. Dessert lovers always save room for the mango tart and the mile-high cheesecake. There's an inside bar and a lounge with pleasant seating arrangements inside and out. *340.774.4262. Villa Olga. D $$*

TUSCAN GRILL

The atmosphere at this tiny air-conditioned place is cozy and sophisticated, with ochre walls decorated with framed art and movie posters, a tiled floor, and a mirrored bar. Settle into one of the two private booths or the four little banquette tables and order wine and a plate of linguini alfredo or linguini puttanesca or sweet Italian sausage mixed with peppers, onions, and mushrooms over bowties. Or choose a little pizza, veal piccata, or a grilled steak. This restaurant shares a kitchen with Epernay (*see page 36*) and some menu items are the same in both places. The difference is that here you will find more Italian dishes and at Epernay more Asian-inspired dishes plus sushi. Luncheon salads and sandwiches are excellent. *Dinner until 11 p.m.; Fri., Sat. until midnight. 340.776.4211. Closed Sun. No lunch Sat. Frenchtown Mall. LD $$*

COMPASS POINT

DOTTIE'S FRONT PORCH

This well-kept secret is a fine place to go for a casual dinner of Swedish meatballs, Mexican lasagna, meat loaf, Thai-style chicken, and pecan chocolate pie. Dottie is in the kitchen nightly and the blackboard at the entrance details the evening's specials. Plastic tables are in a little courtyard hidden by white latticework and decorated with tiny white lights. *Compass Point Marina. No phone. D $-$$*

PATRICK'S

Walls are green and pink and the high ceiling is crossed by heavy wood beams in this peaceful, dimly-lit, air-conditioned dining room. Murals of Caribbean greenery mirror the tropical plants scattered here and there between the tables. The menu combines contemporary with classic. Start with a spinach and ricotta ravioli or a salmon duet (fresh pate and smoked) or coquilles St. Jacques or a lettuce wedge with Maytag blue cheese. Then consider a seared tuna steak over a mirepoix of vegetables and lentils or pork tenderloin encrusted wtih pepper and raspberry jam or beef Wellington or mussels marina with capellini or a smoked strip steak over smashed potatoes. The long bar with upholstered seats is a fine place to belly up for a before-dinner drink. *Reservations for dinner essential in season. Closed Sun. 340.715.3655. Compass Point Marina. D $$*

EAST END RESTAURANTS

AGAVE TERRACE

Dining here is on a little terrace or in a breezy room with open walls. Seafood is the specialty at this popular restaurant, which can be extremely busy, especially on-season. Your server will inform you of the day's choice of catches—four or five fresh fish daily—prepared grilled, pan-fried, blackened, poached, or baked. If you've spent the day on a deep-sea fishing trip, they'll be more than happy to prepare your catch. The menu also includes grilled steaks, a grilled chicken breast, and a handful of pasta dishes. The view of St. John and the British Virgin Islands from the terrace and the bar is truly spectacular. *Reservations necessary. 340.775.4142. East End on Smith Bay Road at Point Pleasant Resort. D $$*

AZURE

Tucked into the hillside in Sapphire Village is this small and casual eatery. Tables are inside, with windows open to the breezes, and outside on a terrace around a small swimming pool. The food is skillfully prepared. For lunch try the Caesar salad with blackened chicken or the pork egg rolls with a spicy Thai dipping sauce or a blackened chicken sandwich with blue cheese or a burger and fries. Dinner entrees include chicken piccata; grilled steaks; duck breasts on stir-fried vegetables with hoisin sauce; and a mixed grill of garlic shrimp, jerked scallops, and lemon-herb catch of the day. Thursday nights features Thai cuisine and Friday is prime rib night. *340.777.4280. Sapphire Village Condos. LD $$*

MOLLY MALONE'S

This eatery is extremely casual and very popular with locals, yachties, and vacationers both day and night. It faces the American Yacht Harbor and your view is of a huge array of boats tied up at slips. There's a large, open-air bar with six TVs and tables are scattered about, some with umbrellas. Despite the name, much more than Irish items are on the menu. So drop by for a fish 'n chips or shepherd's pie or a cheeseburger or a Philly cheese steak or barbecued ribs or a steak. Or just stop by the bar for an icy brew or a frozen island drink. *340.775.1270. American Yacht Harbor, Red Hook. BLD $-$$*

OFF THE HOOK

A long, open hallway leads out to this al fresco restaurant, where casual tables are placed on a broad terrace overlooking the American Yacht Harbor Marina. Come here to enjoy the soft ocean breezes and dine on fresh fish. Try the local yellowtail snapper roasted in banana leaves with creole sauce, or blackened mahi mahi with asparagus hash, or seared tuna with wasabi mashed potatoes. There's also a penne with a basil cream sauce and a filet mignon with sauce au poivre. Starters include tuna tartare, fried calamari, jerk chicken skewers, and a conch and seafood callalloo. *Reservations necessary in season. 340.775.6350. Red Hook. D $$-$$$*

ROMANO'S

Don't miss Romano's. This is **the place** on-season and reservations are a must to dine at Tony Romano's swank northern Italian restaurant. Fresh flowers are on the table and the service is professional at this slightly bright, very upscale delight. The menu is classic (and-not-so-classic, but equally delicious) northern Italian. Lingua di Bue Brasta (veal tongue) and Ossobucco are the most popular dishes here. The roasted carrot soup and the artichoke puree with mushrooms and penne pasta are superb. Look for Tony. He's usually working hard in the kitchen, but he often wanders out toward the end of the evening to greet his guests. This is one of the most popular restaurants on St. Thomas and you may have to wait a bit on-season, even with a reservation. There's a little terrace where you can have a drink but it's far more interesting to sit at the bar and check out the huge number of interesting spirits and grappas that crowd the shelves. Check out the paintings and watercolors adorning the walls. Some are by artists Tony discovers in the Dominican Republic. Others are by Tony himself, who, in addition to being a great chef is also an acclaimed artist. (If you were lucky, you may have caught his one-man show in Manhattan). Cigar lovers will want to try a Tony Romano smoke, or even take some home in the handsome box. This truly is a restaurant you do not want to miss. *Closed Sun. 340.775.0045. Coral World Rd., Smith Bay. D $$-$$$*

ST. THOMAS RITZ-CARLTON GREAT BAY GRILL

If you are looking for a special place to celebrate an anniversary, wanting a quiet and romantic venue to pop the question, or are just in the mood to dress up, the Great Bay Grill is the perfect destination. It's by far the most elegant and stateside-like restaurant on St. Thomas. Tables set with crisp linens and signature blue stemware are in several intimate, air-conditioned dining rooms. The service is predictably gracious and the presentation refined. Perhaps lobster bisque or a shrimp cocktail with papaya mango salsa to begin, followed by baby red snapper baked in a banana leaf or ahi tuna or a filet mignon. The Sunday brunch is classy, with station after station of exquisitely-arranged delights and an entire room devoted to desserts. *Reservations essential. Closed Mon.-Wed. Brunch only Sun. 340.775.3333. 6900 Great Bay. D $$$*

WHALE OF A TALE

Upstairs, right above Molly Malone's, locals and visitors stop in for a casual dinner of seafood: clams, fresh local fish, Caribbean lobster, Maryland crab cakes. There are also chicken dishes and a number of pasta dishes on the menu. Tables are inside and on a terrace and open doors along the walls invite the tropical breezes. *340.775.1270. American Yacht Harbor, Red Hook. D $$*

NORTH SHORE RESTAURANTS
OLD STONE FARM HOUSE

The setting is magnificent. This beautiful stone house was originally a sugar plantation Great House two centuries ago and it's the perfect setting for an elegant restaurant. Three rooms with hardwood floors are separated by stunning stone walls with broad and gracious archways. The inspired menu is contemporary and creative and quite varied. For appetizers, you might start with Prince Edward Island mussels steeped in bass ale and coconut, or truffle parmesan risotto with shaved asparagus, or pan-seared scallops with rosemary and sweet garlic puree. Then you might choose salmon with arugula, mint, and pistachios with a yellow split pea puree and basil tossed pommes frites; or a bacon-wrapped red snapper with caraway roasted Yukon potatoes; or three-day mango Asian duck with miso hazelnut rice and ginger plum wine sauce; or three-cheese ravioli with a tomato anise broth. Or select from the full sushi menu. Come early for a beverage in the romantic courtyard complete with fountain. *Reservations necessary. Closed Mon. 340.777.6277. Rte. 42 at Mahogany Run. D $$-$$$*

SOME GREAT BAKERIES, DELIS, AND TAKE-OUT FOOD

Havensight
Cream and Crumbs Shop (*340.774.2499*), which is in Havensight, features freshly ground coffee, tasty pastries, and rolls.

Frenchtown
Frenchtown Deli (*340.776.7211*) makes great sandwiches (create your own or choose from the list on the board), and you can buy cold sodas; a wide variety of beer and ales; cheeses; pates; knockwurst, bratwurst, and andouille sausage; various salads; and freshly-baked breads.

Red Hook
Grateful Deli (*340.775.5160*), across from the American Yacht Harbor complex, has interesting and unusual sandwiches plus a vegetarian menu.

Cold Stone Creamery (*340.777.2777*), at the American Yacht Harbor, is hard to pass up if you have any interest at all in ice cream. The ice cream here is made fresh daily and flavors can be combined into "Creations"—see the blackboard for a list of the featured combinations of the day, or be creative and choose an exotic combo of your own making. You can get shakes, smoothies, and sundaes, too.

Burrito Bay Deli (*340.775.2944*) makes great traditional sandwiches—ham, tuna, roast beef.

Marina Market (*340.779.2411*) is the best market on St. Thomas and also has excellent food to go. Come and get a salad or pick up dinner for the whole family.

TAXIS AND TAXI DRIVERS

Taxis in St. Thomas can range from compact cars that hold just a few passengers, to large old station wagons that can accommodate a medium-size family plus luggage, to vans and open-air safari buses that can carry close to 20 people.

It is the custom in St. Thomas (and many other islands) to fill up the taxi with people before heading off.

People from the mainland are generally "in a hurry" and can think it's a waste of their vacation time to be made to wait for other people. There is another point of view. Consider, for example, that an islander sees not filling the van as a waste of space (empty seats), a waste of fuel (making the trip twice), and lost income. Plus, what's the hurry?

TAXI TIPS

❑If you are planning to get a taxi from the airport, you'll discover that this is a good time to begin practicing your adjustment to "island time." You'll find that vans sometimes even "wait for the next plane" (which actually won't be that long, since it is probably already on the ground). Hurrying won't get you to your final destination any sooner, and since you have probably already been traveling (including waiting time) from somewhere between four and 17 hours, what's another 15 minutes? Feel and breathe the air and look around. If you are alone or with one or two others and want to head to your destination immediately, look for cab that is almost full. But the best thing to do is to go have a beer at the bar near the luggage carousel and then go get in a cab. You'll most likely find your planemates inside, waiting!

❑If you are in Charlotte Amalie and want to go to Havensight, the quickest way is to look for a fairly full van or safari bus where the driver is calling, "Back to the ship." Just hop on and tell the driver you want to go to the Havensight shops.

❑At hotels, taxis wait in line, and the hotel or doorman will fill taxis with people heading to similar destinations. This can be a good way to meet people and share information.

❑Don't be shy about taking the front seat next to the driver of your taxi. He or she will be pleased. Do buckle up. It's the law in St. Thomas, and taken very seriously.

❑If you get a chance, converse with the taxi drivers. They are generally not only kind but very interesting people. Some have lived on St. Thomas for years and can tell you stories about St. Thomas long ago. Many grew up on other Caribbean islands—Tortola in the BVI, St. Kitts, Antigua, Dominica. You'll also find out that many of the drivers have had numerous careers and lived for long periods in Hartford, Connecticut, or New York City, or Omaha.

❑If you call to have a taxi pick you up, you'll be given the number of the taxi that will come and get you. This number is also the taxi license number so it's easy to know if the taxi headed your way is actually "yours."

❑Taxi fares are regulated and the yellow *St. Thomas This Week* prints these fares. The rates in parentheses are for **each** passenger traveling to the same destination. Keep this list with you and agree on the fare with the driver before you leave. Most drivers are honest and helpful but a few do try to take advantage. The telephone number for the Taxi Lost and Found is 340.776.8294.

For a list of taxi drivers' phone numbers, see page 139.

THE OLD AIRPORT

Travelers who first headed to St. Thomas before the early '90s remember a completely different airport—rustic perhaps, but chock full of character, and with a long, long walk to the plane. Those who know both airports might enjoy the following story.

AN ISLAND STORY

We have this friend. He lived in New York, but his heart belonged to the Virgin Islands. Several times a year for over two decades the St. Thomas Airport was the gateway to the islands he loved so much.

Each time he de-planed and made that long walk to the WWII hangar that was the terminal building, he made his first stop in what to him was a very special place.

This place had no resemblance to "Rick's" and was unquestionably the opposite of "A Clean Well-Lighted Place." This place was that weary, dark, stale-smelling Sparky's Airport Bar.

Our friend wasn't even much of a drinker, but through the years a cold Sparky's Heineken became almost sacramental. It was the phone booth where his mind slipped out of its three-piece suit and into an island shirt.

Finally, after years of just visiting, he and the wife he loved so much were actually moving—taking up residence in these beautiful islands. A dream come true, as they say.

The plane landed at dusk and it was very crowded. The man and his wife entered the terminal from a strange direction. Things seemed different in the airport. Our friend was a little disoriented so he snagged a skycap. "Sorry, how would I get to Sparky's from here?" he asked.

"Sparky's finish, mon. This terminal all new. Progress, don't ya know."

Time stopped for a second or two. Then our friend turned to his wife . . . smiled . . . and said, "That's okay. No problem. I wasn't really that thirsty."

He didn't fool her.

—Reprinted from *The Best of the Peter Island Morning Sun*

CHAPTER 3

GREAT ST. THOMAS WINE BARS, QUIET BARS, LIVELY BARS

"'Twas a woman who
drove me to drink,
and I never had
the courtesy
to thank her for it."
—*W.C. Fields*

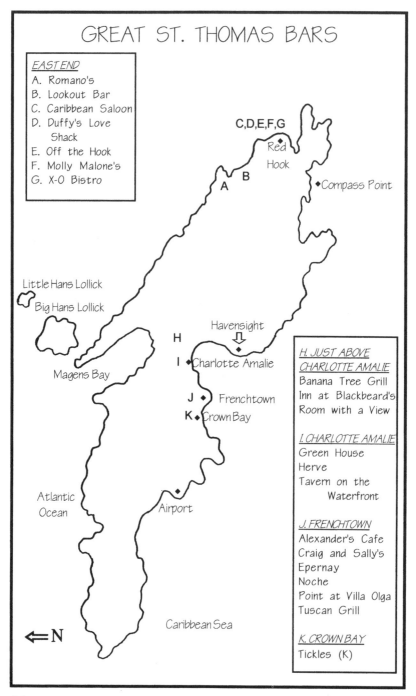

GREAT ST. THOMAS BARS

EAST END
A. Romano's
B. Lookout Bar
C. Caribbean Saloon
D. Duffy's Love Shack
E. Off the Hook
F. Molly Malone's
G. X-O Bistro

C,D,E,F,G
Red Hook

Compass Point

A   B

Little Hans Lollick
Big Hans Lollick

Magens Bay

Havensight

H
I • Charlotte Amalie

J • Frenchtown
K • Crown Bay

Atlantic Ocean

Airport

Caribbean Sea

N

H. JUST ABOVE CHARLOTTE AMALIE
Banana Tree Grill
Inn at Blackbeard's
Room with a View

I. CHARLOTTE AMALIE
Green House
Herve
Tavern on the Waterfront

J. FRENCHTOWN
Alexander's Cafe
Craig and Sally's
Epernay
Noche
Point at Villa Olga
Tuscan Grill

K. CROWN BAY
Tickles (K)

GREAT ST. THOMAS WINE BARS, QUIET BARS, LIVELY BARS

St. Thomas is home to classy bars, casual bars, intimate bars, and noisy bars. Some specialize in fine wines, rare single-malts, and aged ports. Some feature live entertainment. Where the action is changes somewhat, depending on the season. Check St. Thomas This Week *and the Weekend Section in the Thursday edition of the* St. Thomas Daily News *for what is going on when you are on the island.*

CHARLOTTE AMALIE BARS

GREEN HOUSE

If you are going out at night, downtown, you'll probably end up at the Green House sooner or later. It seems everyone does. There is always some party or promotion or "happening" here. It might be Margarita Mondays or Two For Tuesdays or the great band P'Your Passion which plays soca and reggae until 2 a.m. on Fridays. You can even win up to $1,000 on Saturday nights. There are also pool tables and fooz ball in the back and the Green House gets all the stateside sporting events on large screen TVs. Check the *St. Thomas Daily News* for up-to-the-minute schedules here. They also serve food: salads, pizza, pasta, ribs, burgers, and chicken from late morning until 10 p.m. *340.774.7998. Waterfront Hwy.*

HERVE

Upholstered chairs line the wide bar at this sophisticated restaurant and this is a delightful place to come for a quiet drink or perhaps a glass of wine. Check out the excellent wine list. There are over 20 wines available by the glass. *340.777.9703. Government Hill.*

TAVERN ON THE WATERFRONT

In the center of this restaurant is a handsome, square, mahogany bar that is usually buzzing. The bar serves all kinds of mixed and frozen drinks, but if you're a beer drinker, check out their icy-cold assortment from around the world. *Closed Sun. 340.776.4328. Waterfront Hwy.*

BARS JUST ABOVE CHARLOTTE AMALIE

BANANA TREE GRILL

There's a quiet bar in the back of this elegant restaurant and it's a pleasant spot to relax over a drink. And why not just make reservations and stay for dinner? *Closed Mon. 340.776.4050. Bluebeard's Castle on Bluebeard's Hill.*

INN AT BLACKBEARD'S CASTLE LOUNGE

Guests settle back in the comfortable rattan chairs and sofas or gather at the L-shaped bar in this al fresco setting and enjoy champagne by the glass, or single malt scotches, or martinis. The bar menu contains many of the salads and appetizers on the restaurant menu. You might try Voodoo steamed shrimp with lime-cilantro cocktail sauce, jerk-spiced fried calamari with Latin-style remoulade, or penne puttanesca. *Closed Sun. 340.776.1234. Government Hill.*

ROOM WITH A VIEW

Floor-to-ceiling windows showcase a fabulous view of Charlotte Amalie and sunsets and nighttime scenes are wonderfully romantic. There's a long wine list, including many by the glass and a chalkboard by the bar lists daily wine and appetizer specials. There's a complete dinner menu (*see page 35*). After-dinner cordials and specialty coffees and great desserts (Godiva chocolate cheesecake, chocolate sundaes) make this an excellent end-of-the-evening stop if you've already dined next door at the Banana Tree Grill or elsewhere on the island. *Closed Sun. 340.774.2377. Bluebeard's Castle, Bluebeard Hill.*

FRENCHTOWN BARS

ALEXANDER'S CAFE

The bar at the back of this classy restaurant is a popular gathering spot for locals and vacationers alike. *Closed Sun. 340.774.4349.*

CRAIG AND SALLY'S

This popular Frenchtown restaurant has a busy and congenial bar with seating on two sides and it fills up fast. They have a full bar but be sure to inquire about the wines by the glass. There are many, and numerous unusual ones. You can dine at the bar if you want. *Closed Mon.-Tues. 340.777.9949.*

EPERNAY

At this very dark and intimate bar and bistro, an interesting selection of champagnes and red and white wines of the evening are scrawled on the blackboard and there's a long list of cognacs, armagnacs, Spanish brandies, single-malt scotches, and ports by the glass. There's a small bar and cozy tables line the wall. A delightful dinner is served here, too (*see page 36*). *Closed Sun. 340.774.5348.*

NOCHE

Margaritas are the specialty at this lively bar and lounge at the entrance to this classy Spanish and South American restaurant. Or you might sample one of the many premium tequilas. *340.774.3800.*

POINT AT VILLA OLGA
Inside, settle into a rattan love seat or belly up to the comfortable bar or head to a table outside along the narrow terrace and enjoy the soft sea breezes and twinkling nighttime sky. This could be the time to try a real island drink, like a frozen strawberry margarita or an icy pina colada. *340.774.4262.*

TICKLES
It's not really in Frenchtown, but actually the next bay west, at Crown Bay Marina, which is also where you catch the ferry to Water Island (the dock is just to the side of the restaurant). This is a great open-air bar with wonderful water views and good casual fare, like burgers and fries. Locals flock here day and night and for the always popular happy hour. *340.776.1595. Crown Bay Marina.*

TUSCAN GRILL
This is a small restaurant and the bar is quiet but comfortable. You can dine at the bar if you want (*see menu page 37*). *Closed Sun. 340.776.4211.*

EAST END BARS
CARIBBEAN SALOON
The bar is big and busy here and popular with young and old alike. In fact many of the bartenders and wait staff that work at this end of the island hang here at the end of their day (which can be late in the evening) and the menu of burgers, fries, buffalo wings, and meatball subs is served from 11 a.m. until 4. am. *340.775.7060. American Yacht Harbor. Red Hook.*

DUFFY'S LOVE SHACK
The draw at this casual, funky establishment is the mix of icy cold beers, tasty frozen drinks, lots of people, and rock and roll music turned up high. They serve food here, too. *340.779.2080. Red Hook.*

LOOKOUT BAR
The seats are lined up to give you one of the very best views of St. John and the nearby British Virgin Islands. The sun sets in the opposite direction but sunsets are still beautiful here. If you want to avoid the crowds waiting for dinner at the popular adjoining Agave Terrace restaurant, walk past the bar to the tiny outside terrace. *340.775.4142. Point Pleasant Resort, Smith Bay Rd.*

MOLLY MALONE'S
The large bar is open to the breezes and the scenery is boats everywhere in the busy marina. Belly up to the bar and swap stories with yachties, locals, and vacationers with an icy-cold beer. *340.775.1270. American Yacht Harbor.*

OFF THE HOOK

The bar is open-air and looks out to the marina and the many boats at dock and is popular with locals. *340.775.6350. Red Hook.*

ROMANO'S

This narrow little bar has comfortable seats and you can spend an hour or two reading the labels on all the bottles of grappa and other interesting spirits and wines that line the wall. Or look the other way and gaze at the wonderful paintings on the walls, some collected by the owner who searches out aspiring artists in the Dominican Republic, and some painted by the owner (Tony Romano), who happens to be an acclaimed artist as well as an award-winning chef. The art is for sale, if something happens to catch your eye. *Closed Sun. 340.775.0045. Smith Bay Rd.*

X-O BISTRO

Champagnes and wines by the glass plus a full bar are the draw at this late night watering hole. *340.779.2069. Red Hook.*

A BEVERAGE UNDER THE STARS

This chapter suggests almost two dozen different venues to enjoy a margarita or martini, a frozen daiquiri or a diet coke. Wonderful choices for a pre-dinner cocktail, a glass of wine, or an after-dinner eau de vie...but one really great choice is missing from the preceding list. That choice is the deck, balcony, terrace, or beach right outside the door to the room or villa where you are staying.

It's peaceful and private. And whether you choose to watch the day melt into evening with a cocktail before dinner or return from dinner and sit sipping under the stars, the experience is one that should definitely not be missed.

ALWAYS . . .

Always be nicer to people than necessary.

Always lock your hotel room and rental car.

Always have a hat, bandanna, or something to cover your head during the day.

Always remember to keep left when you are driving.

Always look right first, and then left before crossing the street.

Always put on some sunscreen before going outside during the day.

Always greet people and ask how they are doing before conducting any "business."

Always remember the sometimes slower pace you encounter is part of the island charm.

Always snorkel with at least one other person.

ST. CROIX FOR THE DAY

St. Croix sits by itself about 40 miles south of St. Thomas so it takes a bit longer to get there than it does to get to most of the other neighboring islands. However, you'll still have enough time to have fun on St. Croix, provided you have something specific in mind—you won't have time to do everything.

You can drive around the island and visit several beaches. **Olympic Car Rental** *rents cars near the dock (340.772.2000), or you can take yourself on an historic walk through downtown Christiansted (directions in the free* St. Croix This Week*).*

You can head out to the Buck Island U.S. National Park (which is different than the Buck Island just off St. Thomas), or you can ride through a rain forest on horseback. Call **Paul and Jill's Equestrian Stables** *(340.772.2880).*

How can you get there? You can take a regular plane or a seaplane or even a ferry. However, please check to see what is running when you are on island. Over the last 15 years plane schedules, seaplane service, and boat transportation between St. Thomas and St. Croix has changed often (and several hydrofoils have come and gone).

BY PLANE

It's a 20- to 30-minute flight and planes leave from the St. Thomas airport. Round-trip, same-day fare is $99. **Cape Air** *(800.352.0714)* flies between St. Thomas and St. Croix several times daily.

BY SEAPLANE

A neat seaplane flies from the Charlotte Amalie Waterfront (at the Marine Terminal, where the ferries leave for the BVI) to right in front of the Best Western hotel in Christiansted. It's a quick 17 minutes in the air. There are several morning flights and, for day-trippers, a convenient afternoon return. Fare is $135. Call **Seaborne Seaplanes** *(340.773.6442)*.

BY FERRY

It takes about an hour and 15 minutes to travel by ferry between St. Thomas and St. Croix. Call **Boston Harbor Cruises Ferry** *(877.733.9425)*, which operates a ferry service from November to May. The fare is $70 round trip.

COVETED CRUZAN BRACELETS

Look for the famous sterling silver Cruzan "hook" bracelets in jewelry stores. There are also earrings and rings. For many years you could only get these if you actually went to St. Croix, but if you run out of time, you can now buy them on St. Thomas at **Elizabeth James** in Red Hook.

ART GALLERIES

(MANY GALLERIES WILL SHIP ANYWHERE YOU WANT)

CHARLOTTE AMALIE

JONNA WHITE GALLERY. Works of local artist Jonna White (Main Street at Royal Dane Mall).

CAMILLE PISSARO ART GALLERY. Originals and prints by local artists (Main Street).

CARIBBEAN PRINT GALLERY. Prints, old maps (on Main Street at A. H. Riise).

VISITORS' HOSPITALITY LOUNGE. Sometimes showcases works by local artists (across from Vendors' Plaza).

AROUND THE ISLAND

TILLET GARDENS. Art of all kinds in galleries and silk-screened fabrics and a restaurant (near Tutu Park).

KILNWORKS POTTERY AND ART GALLERY. A working pottery studio and work by local artists (at Smith Bay, East End).

MANGO TANGO ART GALLERY. Caribbean art, prints, and handcrafts (at Al Cohen Mall on Raphune Hill).

REICHHOLD CENTER GALLERY. Art by local artists (at the University of the Virgin Islands).

CHAPTER 4

GREAT
ST. THOMAS
SHOPPING

"Whoever said money can't buy happiness
didn't know where to shop."

—Anonymous

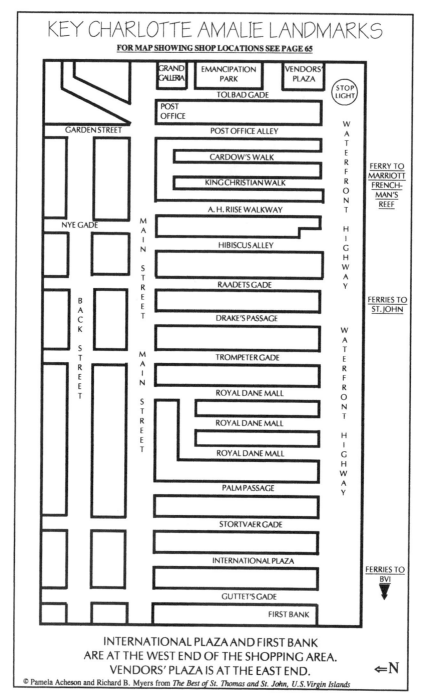

KEY CHARLOTTE AMALIE LANDMARKS

FOR MAP SHOWING SHOP LOCATIONS SEE PAGE 65

GRAND GALLERIA • EMANCIPATION PARK • VENDORS' PLAZA • STOP LIGHT

TOLBAD GADE

POST OFFICE

GARDEN STREET

POST OFFICE ALLEY

CARDOW'S WALK

KING CHRISTIAN WALK

A. H. RIISE WALKWAY

NYE GADE

HIBISCUS ALLEY

RAADETS GADE

DRAKE'S PASSAGE

TROMPETER GADE

ROYAL DANE MALL

ROYAL DANE MALL

ROYAL DANE MALL

PALM PASSAGE

STORTVAER GADE

INTERNATIONAL PLAZA

GUTTET'S GADE

FIRST BANK

MAIN STREET

BACK STREET

WATERFRONT HIGHWAY

FERRY TO MARRIOTT FRENCHMAN'S REEF

FERRIES TO ST. JOHN

WATERFRONT HIGHWAY

FERRIES TO BVI

INTERNATIONAL PLAZA AND FIRST BANK
ARE AT THE WEST END OF THE SHOPPING AREA.
VENDORS' PLAZA IS AT THE EAST END. ⇐ N

© Pamela Acheson and Richard B. Myers from *The Best of St. Thomas and St. John, U.S. Virgin Islands*

SHOPPING IN CHARLOTTE AMALIE
(HAVENSIGHT AND RED HOOK STORES APPEAR AT THE END OF THIS CHAPTER)

Everyone knows that Charlotte Amalie is a world-class duty-free shopping mecca, but what no one ever points out is that there are also wonderful, original shops—intriguing stores even for people who hate to shop—with items you may never find anywhere else tucked here and there in the Charlotte Amalie alleyways.

Charlotte Amalie certainly gets its share of negative comments. People complain that it's too crowded and full of street hawkers. Well, there are hawkers and it can be very crowded when lots of cruise ships are in. Also, the place itself is somewhat confusing, and this is compounded by the throngs of people who can make it difficult to see where you are.

For some, the crowds are part of the fun. But if you want to avoid them, head downtown in mid-afternoon. Many cruise ship shoppers will have returned to their ship and the town can be quite pleasant. It also helps to go when few ships are in (check schedules in St. Thomas This Week*). Certain days off-season no ships are in and town is a delight.*

HOW CHARLOTTE AMALIE IS ORGANIZED
Two main streets are parallel to each other and lined with shops: Waterfront Highway (which runs along the harbor) and Main Street. Numerous narrow alleys (walkways), also lined with shops, connect these two streets. Each alley has a name (often Danish, with letter combinations non-Danish speaking people can find difficult to make sense of). However, you don't really need to know these names because, although you will see these names on maps, a good number of alleys do not have identifying signs anyway.

FINDING YOUR WAY AROUND
So, how do you find anything in this rabbit warren of alleyways with non-pronounceable names that often aren't posted? Easy. People rely on landmarks—just about everything is either near the Post Office, or Vendors' Plaza, or First Bank. Don't be embarrassed if you can't find the store you were just in. Even locals get confused in these alleyways. **See the map on page 65 to locate easily the shops you want to find.**

CHARLOTTE AMALIE SHOPS

The stores below are selected because they have something special to offer. Most aren't "famous" and some are places that very few people know about. They are organized alphabetically by category. Use the numbers next to each shop name to locate it on the map on page 65.

Charlotte Amalie's great duty-free stores—Columbian Emeralds, Royal Caribbean, A.H Riise, Cardow's, and Little Switzerland (the places where you can buy diamonds and gold jewelry, gemstones, crystal, linens, watches, electronics, perfumes, cosmetics, and liquor)— aren't included below because these renowned shops are covered so thoroughly in free tourist information guides like the yellow St. Thomas This Week *and because you can't miss these large shops. By the way, if you are hoping to get a good deal on a specific item, check out the price of the same item in the states and know the exact model number.*

ANTIQUES
CARSON CO. ANTIQUES (24)
Old brick archways provide a tasteful background for these two rooms of antiquities from ancient times through the 19th century. Come to this well-organized shop for old books (some rare), ancient coins, maps, pottery, African masks, estate and ancient jewelry, and a huge stock of Christmas ornaments. *340.774.6175. Northwest end of Royal Dane Mall.*

SHIPWRECK OCEAN SALVAGE ANTIQUES (22)
This is a wonderful shop to explore. The specialty is registered ancient coins from all over the world but the owners also run a salvage shop which is the source of much of what you see. The walls are hung with artwork and old maps of the Caribbean and antique parts of boats are on display and for sale. There are beautiful ship wheels and lanterns, plus old coins (some in pins, pendants, and rings), maps, books on the Caribbean, and even old USVI license plates. A brilliantly colored parrot speaks her mind. *340.774.2074. On Waterfront Hwy. at Royal Dane Mall West.*

ART
MAPes MONDe ART GALLERY (3)
When you tire of the crowds, head to this inviting and peaceful gallery. Spacious rooms are hung with numerous works of art, many of which focus on the historical past of the Caribbean and the U.S. Virgin Islands. There are also prints, maps, and books, circa 1500-1800. Many items are for sale and can be shipped anywhere. *340.776.2886. Grand Galleria.*

MITCH GIBBS (27)

Near the north end of Palm Passage, there's a very informal outdoor stand that showcases the art of Mitch Gibbs. He works in oil, watercolor, pastel, and acrylic and has several distinctive styles, all appealing. Look for incredibly realistic paintings of Caribbean islands, water, waves, sunsets, and clouds. Whatever you choose can be shipped anywhere you please. *No phone. Center of Palm Passage.*

CARIBBEAN ITEMS

CALYPSO, LTD. (11)

There's a tea and cappuccino bar at the back of this unusual gift shop, which includes many Caribbean-made products, and you can sample blends of java while you consider what to buy. There are locally made sauces, jellies from Anegada, jewelry made in St. Thomas and St. John, Caribbean cookbooks, island music, neat children's toys, local spices, skin care products, and coffees and teas. *340.776.2303. Deep inside the A. H. Riise Mall; enter from western entrance on Main St. and walk straight back through the watches.*

CARIBBEAN PRINT GALLERY (9)

Come to this tiny alleyway location for a great selection of greeting cards, stunning books including MAPes MONDe editions, lovely Caribbean maps, and frameable Caribbean watercolors and paintings. They carry poster tubes for easy traveling. This is a popular spot and also somewhat cramped, but worth the stop, so if it's too crowded for you, just come back later in the day. *340.776.2886. On Main St., in the middle of the A. H. Riise building.*

DOWN ISLAND TRADERS (5)

There is much more to this store than the T-shirts and Caribbean teas, coffees, spices, and jams just inside the entrance. Look for a delightful potpourri of island wares—pottery from the St. Thomas Kilnworks, hand-painted Christmas tree ornaments, island artwork, watercolor maps of the Caribbean, cards and watercolors by Flukes of the British Virgin Islands, teas and coffees, greeting cards and cookbooks, beach bags, colorful beach towels, island music, and sterling silver jewelry. *340.776.4641. East end of Waterfront Hwy. shops, just west of Vendors' Plaza.*

CLOTHING (CASUAL)

KALI BOUTIQUE (20)

Hidden away in the middle of Royal Dane Mall is this delight. Look for whimsical purses created out of sequins and colorful fabrics, gauzy tie-dyed dresses and wraps, silky tops, eye-catching sandals, and one-of-a-kind gift items, all artfully displayed. *340.777.4949. Middle of Royal Dane Mall.*

LOCAL COLOR (17)

This is a great place to come for comfortable sundresses and shirts and casual pants and capris in bright island prints. Jams clothing is featured. There are plenty of clothes for kids here, too. *340.774.2280. On Waterfront Hwy. at corner of Royal Dane Mall East.*

PUSSER'S COMPANY STORE (10)

If you haven't yet experienced one of the very popular Pusser's Company stores, now is your chance. They are found all over the U.S. and British Virgin Islands and are one of the best places to shop for comfortable Pusser's sportswear (T-shirts, sweatshirts, caps, shorts, windbreakers, sweaters, and shirts) for the whole family. You'll also find an excellent assortment of island books, watches, tote bags, appealing souvenirs, great gifts, and, naturally, the famous Pusser's Rum, available in interesting decanters as well as standard bottles. *340.777.9281. In the middle of the A. H. Riise Walkway, four alleys west of Vendors' Plaza.*

QUIET STORM (23)

Looking for colorful prints and comfortable clothing? Tommy Bahama shorts, pants, shirts, and sandals for men, and pants, skirts, tops, and outfits for women are displayed just inside the entrance. Head deeper into the store if you are looking for Jams, Axis, Island Paradise, and other well-known brands. *340.774.7588. On Waterfront Hwy. at corner of Palm Passage.*

CLOTHING (DESIGNER)

COSMOPOLITAN (15)

Come here for Gottex, Bally, Paul & Shark, and Burma Bibas labels. There's a great selection of women's swimwear and swimwear cover-ups. There's also swimwear for men and tennis wear for men and women plus men's slacks, shirts, shorts, and accessories—including belts and ties. Be sure to check out the upstairs also. *340.776.2040. On Waterfront Hwy. at Drake's Passage.*

NICOLE MILLER BOUTIQUE (25)

Nicole Miller became famous for her absolutely stunning, delightfully whimsical ties and now, of course, she fashions all manner of things out of these amusing silk prints. They're all available here—umbrellas, dop kits, address books, boxer shorts, swimsuits, bathrobes, vests, jackets, shirts, and ties. Stop here also for Ms. Miller's line of very sexy, feminine clothing—in solids as well as her famous prints. The 1300-square-foot boutique with white marble floors is a cool classy interior to show off Ms. Miller's sensational silk designs. The exceptionally courteous and knowledgeable staff will help you find what you are looking for. *340.774.8286. On Main St. at Palm Passage.*

POLO RALPH LAUREN (28)

Floor-to-ceiling shelves display rows and rows of neatly folded cable sweaters and knit shirts. Rows of long pants, shorts, and bathing suits hang against the wall. And tables display socks, belts, and nicely arranged stacks of colorful clothing. Most of the items are for men but there is a small selection for women. *No phone. Midway into Palm Passage.*

TOMMY HILFIGER (16)

Tommy Hilfiger fans will want to head into this huge store, which has a bit of everything you can imagine, all branded with his famous moniker. *340.777.1189. On Waterfront Hwy. between Royal Dane Mall and Trompeter Gade.*

TUTTO MODA (29)

This sleek and elegant showroom is the perfect display place for chic designer clothes: Versace, Zagini, La Perla, Jiki, and the hottest new designers from France. *340.715.3256. Middle of Palm Passage.*

CHOCOLATES
CARIBBEAN CHOCOLATE COMPANY (26)

This is a chocoholic's super-heaven. You might want to just sniff and savor the Godiva chocolate in the air before getting down to deciding exactly which Godiva truffle you should sample first: double chocolate raspberry, chocolate with Amaretto, french vanilla with Myers's rum, or black cherry? It's okay to go in and just have one single truffle. In fact people do this again and again, all day long. There are also rum balls, rum cakes, sugar-free chocolates, West Indian jellies, Godiva coffees (hot and by the cup as well as packaged), and gourmet jelly beans which you can buy by flavor or choose your own mix. *340.774.6675. On Main Street, connected to the Haagen Dazs shop.*

DRUGSTORE
OTC DRUGSTORE (12)

If you've run out of your favorite shampoo, or want a prescription filled, just walk right through Mr. Tablecloth and up several steps. You'll be in a full-service drugstore. You can even have your stateside doctor phone in a prescription. *340.774.5432. Corner of Main St. and Nye Gade.*

JEWELRY AND SCULPTURES
OKIDANOKH GOLDCRAFT (19)

Arched doorways, brick walls, and fanciful illustrations of unicorns and hot air balloons create a peaceful setting for display tables showcasing finely handcrafted gold and silver jewelry. Look for delicate, very original earrings, necklaces, bracelets, and pendants. *340.774.9677. Back of Royal Dane Mall.*

BERNARD K. PASSMAN GALLERY (7)

This is a remarkable store and gallery showcasing exquisite pieces of jewelry and delicate small black coral sculptures by world-famous Bernard Passman: a miniature piano with all 88 keys ($22,000); a drum set complete with cymbals and several miniature drums—look for the swirls on the drums, which are the natural swirls in the coral ($28,000); a delicate image of a can-can girl with 22-karat gold boots ($175,000). Perhaps the most famous is that of Charlie Chaplin, with his dog—in solid gold—next to him. It's been valued at $1.2 million. So, what can a regular person afford? Beautiful gold and black coral bracelets, striking diamond and black coral rings, and lovely pendants in the shape of fish with gold eyes. Prices start at $60 and every single piece is exquisitely detailed and initialed. The sales people treat the place as an art gallery and are very warm and friendly and will happily explain the interesting histories behind the more famous pieces even if you are just a browser. *340.777.4580. On Main St., one block west of the Post Office.*

LINGERIE

LOVER'S LANE (13)

Follow the narrow stairs up to this hedonistic den of lingerie and adult pleasures. Pick out some sexy underwear, or exotic swimwear, or find a romantic gift. *340.777.9616. Waterfront Hwy. between Raadet's Gade and Hibiscus Alley.*

SHOES AND SANDALS

SHOE TREE (6)

This is an excellent spot for brand name ladies' shoes. You'll find a good selection of sandals, comfortable flats, and dressy heels. Check out the sale shoes on the floor by the cash register. There's almost always at least one great bargain. *340.774.3900. On Cardow's Walk, just beyond the entrance to Bumpa's Cafe.*

ZORA'S (1)

Zora's has been here since 1962 and people come from all over the world for custom-made leather sandals that are exquisitely comfortable and last close to forever. There are also ready-made sandals, canvas bags, famous limin' shoes, Great Wall of China backpacks, kids' canvas shark and fish purses, belly bags, and monster backpacks that look, well, just like monsters. If you want custom-made sandals, it takes five days so head here on your first or second day of vacation to get measured and to chose a style (there are at least 50, named after nifty places on nearby islands, like Joe's Hill on Tortola). Before you head home you can stop in for a final fitting and to get your sandals. Zora, her daughters, and Ann are caring craftspeople. Be sure to take one of their catalogues home with you. That way, when you get home and wish you'd bought that neat cat bag, or want to order another pair of limin' shoes, or decide you want to do all your Christmas shopping at Zora's, you can! *340.774.2559. From the Post Office walk east on Main St. Go over the little hill and look for the stoplight in the distance. The store is on the right, just before the stoplight.*

SWIM AND BEACH WEAR
DEL SOL (2, 14, 21)

Stuff may look a bit dull inside this shop but take anything here into the sun and then watch out! Like magic, black and white or blue and white designs on T-shirts, beach bags, beach towels, swim trunks, and more transform into a riot of color! And there's more. Nail polish switches from one vivid shade to another. Sunglasses completely change shades. Markers (the kind you draw with) go from one color to another. It's so cool! *340.774.2753. Three locations: The largest store is on Waterfront Hwy. between Drake's Passage and Raadets Gade. A tiny store is four blocks to the west on Waterfront Hwy. A mid-size store is in the Grand Galleria.*

GOING SEANILE (18)

It beats getting old! If you can use it near water, you'll probably find what you need in this little shop for sunning and beach needs, from sunglasses to sandals, reef shoes, visor hats, bathing suits, swim trunks, and T-shirts, many showing off their wacky logo. *340.774.1510. Waterfront at Royal Dane Mall East.*

TAPES AND CDs
SAM GOODY (8)

For the hottest and latest tapes and compact discs and for swing, alternative music, soft and hard rock, easy listening, classical music, oldies—whatever you seek, you'll probably find it in this large upstairs store. There are videos, too. *340.774.8092. Upstairs on Main St. just west of Garden St.*

VISITORS' HOSPITALITY LOUNGE
VISITORS' HOSPITALITY LOUNGE (4)

Many visitors don't know that there is a wonderful hospitality lounge run by volunteers that is just for you! Stop here and rest your feet or use the restroom. Settle into a chair and browse through brochures on what to do and where to go. You can even leave your luggage here (there's a small charge per piece). And please leave a donation. *340.777.8827. Across from Vendors' Plaza.*

FOR A MAP SHOWING THE LOCATION OF SHOPS DESCRIBED HERE, JUST TURN THE PAGE

SHOPS IN CHARLOTTE AMALIE
SEE MAP FOR LOCATION

ANTIQUES
Carson Co. Antiques (24)
Shipwreck Ocean Salvage (22)

ART
MAPes MONDe (3)
Mitch Gibbs (27)

CARIBBEAN ITEMS
Calypso (11)
Caribbean Print Gallery (9)
Down Island Traders (5)

CLOTHING (CASUAL)
Kali Boutique (20)
Local Color (17)
Pusser's Company Store (10)
Quiet Storm (23)

CLOTHING (DESIGNER)
Cosmopolitan (15)
Nicole Miller Boutique (25)
Polo Ralph Lauren (28)
Tommy Hilfiger (16)
Tutto Moda (29)

CHOCOLATES
Caribbean Chocolate Co. (26)

DRUGSTORE
OTC (12)

JEWELRY AND SCULPTURES
Okidanokh Goldcraft (19)
Bernard K. Passman Gallery (7)

LINGERIE
Lover's Lane (13)

SHOES & SANDALS
Shoe Tree (6)
Zora's (1)

SWIM AND BEACH WEAR
Cosmopolitan (15)
Del Sol (2, 14, 21)
Going Seanile (18)

TAPES & CDS
Sam Goody (8)

**VISITORS'
HOSPITALITY LOUNGE (4)**

1. Zora's
2. Del Sol
3. MAPes MONDe
4. Visitors' Lounge
5. Down Island Traders
6. Shoe Tree
7. Bernard K. Passman
8. Sam Goody
9. Caribbean Print Gallery
10. Pusser's
11. Calypso
12. OTC
13. Lover's Lane
14. Del Sol
15. Cosmopolitan
16. Tommy Hilfiger
17. Local Color
18. Going Seanile
19. Okidanokh Goldcraft
20. Kali Boutique
21. Del Sol
22. Shipwreck Ocean Sal.
23. Quiet Storm
24. Carson Co. Antiques
25. Nicole Miller
26. Caribbean Chocolate
27. Mitch Gibbs
28. Polo Ralph Lauren
29. Tutto Moda

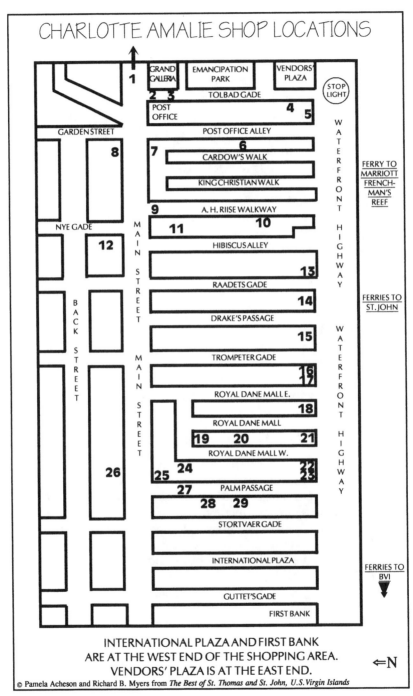

CHARLOTTE AMALIE SHOP LOCATIONS

INTERNATIONAL PLAZA AND FIRST BANK
ARE AT THE WEST END OF THE SHOPPING AREA.
VENDORS' PLAZA IS AT THE EAST END.

⇐N

© Pamela Acheson and Richard B. Myers from *The Best of St. Thomas and St. John, U.S. Virgin Islands*

HAVENSIGHT SHOPPING

Havensight was built to make it easy for cruise ship passengers to shop without having to go anywhere. Original shops and small branches of many of the duty-free Charlotte Amalie stores are located here in long one-story buildings that stretch back from the cruise ship dock. Also here is the red-roofed Ports of Sale complex. Havensight is never really that crowded and this is an easy place to check out duty-free bargains whether or not you are on a cruise ship and if you don't want to go to town. Many of these shops will be closed if no ships are in.

DOCKSIDE BOOKSHOP

For a superb selection of books in the best bookstore in the Virgin Islands, head straight here. You'll find two floors loaded with hard- and soft-cover best sellers, shelves and shelves of novels, mysteries, and adventures, plus books on travel, hobbies, cookbooks, and more. Check out the shelf to the right of the cash register for wonderful books on St. Thomas, the Virgin Islands, and the whole Caribbean. *340.774.4937. Havensight Mall.*

MODERN MUSIC

Across the street from Havensight is this great tape and CD store. Come here for the latest stateside releases plus loads of island music, including albums by Bankie Banx, a terrific recording star from Anguilla. *340.774.3100. Across the street from Havensight's main entrance.*

ST. THOMAS' BEST MARKET

MARINA MARKET IN RED HOOK

This is absolutely the best market on St. Thomas. Come here for really fresh produce—red and yellow peppers, portobello mushrooms, yellow tomatoes, numerous lettuces; for excellent wines and champagnes; for specialty items; for a great assortment of upscale stateside brand grocery items; and for a truly great butcher—place your custom order or choose marinated chicken breasts, small rack of lamb, whole tenderloins, or ground sirloin. Come here also for excellently prepared food to go—homemade mashed potatoes, grilled chicken, and a great salad bar. Take it home or eat outside on the little terrace. *340.779.2411.*

RED HOOK SHOPPING

Red Hook is located at the east end of St. Thomas. If you are staying on this end of the island, or if you are planning to catch the Red Hook ferry to St. John, you might want to check out one or all of these interesting Red Hook shops. All are on the first floor of the American Yacht Harbor complex.

CHRIS SAWYER DIVING STORE

In addition to diving gear, there are bathing suits, sunglasses, hats, sandals, snorkel gear, and a good selection of postcards. *340.777.7804.*

DOLPHIN DREAMS BOUTIQUE

The display windows of this appealing shop are sure to catch your eye. The entrance is actually around the corner. Stop here for hand-painted glassware, island music CDs, books, prints by local artists, handmade soaps, colorful pottery, purses, casual shirts for men and women, gauzy island dresses, and numerous other items. *340.775.0549.*

ELIZABETH JAMES

In this appealing jewelry and clothing boutique, lovely silver bracelets and necklaces and earrings are displayed. Need something to wear with your new bracelet? Check out the washable silk scoop tops, linen and silk blouses, and the selections of Flax clothing: soft comfortable shirts, pants, shorts, and tops. This is also a place to buy the famous Crucian Hook bracelet that is made in St. Croix as well as Crucian Hook earrings and rings. *340.779.1595.*

KEEP LEFT

Stop here for a huge array of island, resort, and warm weather wear for the whole family. You don't necessarily have to keep left, but do keep walking. There's lots to see in this large shop. Look for dresses and capri pants and shirts by Jams. You'll find shorts, bathing suits, shirts, and shoes by Patagonia and Quicksilver. *340.775.9964.*

RHIANNON'S

Glittery and magical fairy dust that you can scatter about for good luck is just one of the delightful things you will find in this New Age store. Stunning quilts by local artists hang on the walls. Tables display spell boxes, good quality incense sticks, a huge array of candles, wonderful books of all sizes, and so much more. There are also delicate earrings, bracelets, and necklaces. If you'd like a tarot reading, just make an appointment. *340.779.1877.*

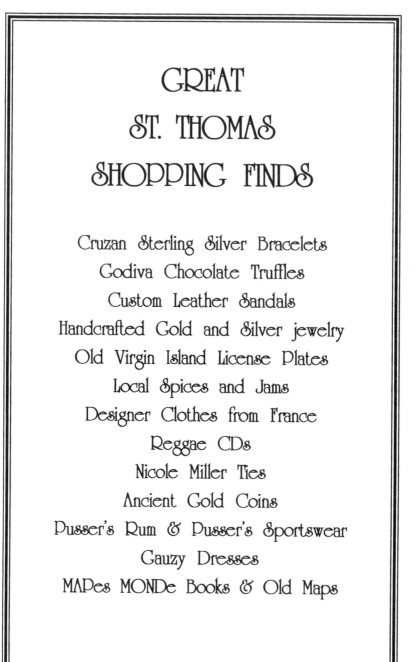

GREAT ST. THOMAS SHOPPING FINDS

Cruzan Sterling Silver Bracelets
Godiva Chocolate Truffles
Custom Leather Sandals
Handcrafted Gold and Silver jewelry
Old Virgin Island License Plates
Local Spices and Jams
Designer Clothes from France
Reggae CDs
Nicole Miller Ties
Ancient Gold Coins
Pusser's Rum & Pusser's Sportswear
Gauzy Dresses
MAPes MONDe Books & Old Maps

GREAT THINGS TO LOOK FOR

THE BIRDS YOU WERE FEEDING LAST SUMMER
Don't be surprised if some of the birds you see look a lot like the songbirds you had in your backyard last summer. They head here from North America every winter, too. Some actually go all the way to South America, stopping here on the way down and on the way back north.

HITCHHIKING BIRDS
If you take a ferry anywhere, look to see if a bird seems to "hang in the air" close to the boat. It'll be a Brown Booby, hitching a ride. You'll see them actually search out a power boat so they can catch a ride in the boat's air wake. If they spot a fish, they'll swoop right down and catch it and then race like crazy to catch back up to the boat to continue their "extra-easy" ride.

HOMEMADE FREIGHTERS
Head down to the Charlotte Amalie waterfront and walk along the harbor until you see some small cargo boats. Stop and read the handmade signs in front of some of the vessels: "Will take cargo to Dominica, Guadaloupe, and St. Lucia" or "Leaving for Sint Maarten tonight." These small boats travel from island to island, often carrying bananas or other produce north to St. Thomas and bringing much-needed freight back to some of the southern Caribbean islands.

LOCAL KNOWLEDGE

PERFUME DEALS
You can get great deals on cosmetics and perfumes not only while you are on St. Thomas, but even after you return home. Simply call **A. H. Riise** at 800.524.2037 and place your order.

RECYCLED BALLAST
Many of the bricks used in the buildings on St. Thomas were originally used simply as ballast on the ships that came to St. Thomas to pick up cargo. These ships dumped the bricks and filled their hulls with rum and sugar and returned to Europe.

GETTING LOST
Don't feel stupid if you can't find the store you were in five minutes ago when you are shopping in Charlotte Amalie. This happens to everyone—including people who have lived on St. Thomas for years.

OPENING DAYS
Some restaurants are closed on Sundays . . . several on Mondays, and a few on Tuesdays. But also the days may change at different times of the year. It's probably best to call first on these days or nights.

DOMINOS
You can play dominos or whist every Wednesday and Saturday night at **Percy's Bus Stop**. If you're interested, call Percy at 340.774.5993.

CHAPTER 5

GREAT CHARLOTTE AMALIE LUNCH BREAKS

"Ask not what you can do for your country.
Ask what's for lunch."

—Orson Welles

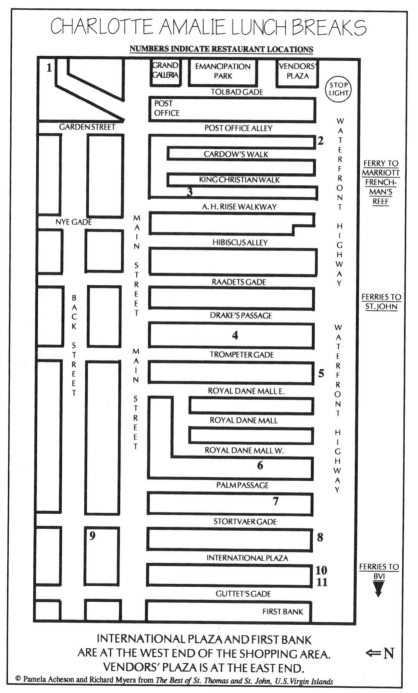

© Pamela Acheson and Richard Myers from *The Best of St. Thomas and St. John, U.S. Virgin Islands*

GREAT CHARLOTTE AMALIE LUNCH BREAKS

There are many places along the waterfront or tucked in alleyways in between shops where you can pause and have breakfast or lunch or a snack or just a cool beverage. These spots are generally open from about 7:30 a.m. to 4 or 5 p.m., although some stay open later in season. Those that don't serve breakfast open around 11a.m. Directions at the end of each description correlate to the map at left.

AMALIA CAFE/MESSON AMALIA (7)
Two rows of tables dressed with white linens are set on a narrow terrace rimmed with flower boxes and a wrought iron railing. The menu is decidedly Spanish. Grilled shrimp, sauteed garlic mushrooms, baby eels Bilbania-style, and grilled vegetables with anchovies are just some of the tapas offered. There are also salads, paella Valenciana, and red snapper in brandy sauce, and the lunch menu includes a roasted pork loin baguette. *Closed Sun. 340.714.7373. Palm Passage. LD $-$$*

BOBBY'S (4)
Tables are close together and it can often look too crowded at Bobby's but once you're seated, it's okay. Stop by for good Caesar salad with grilled chicken, taco salad, hamburgers, pizza, barbecued pork tenderloin sandwich, and their homemade veggie burger. *340.774.6054. Entrances on both Trompeter Gade and Drake's Passage. L $*

BUMPA'S (2)
This outdoor, second-floor cafe is a place to escape the hustle and bustle below. Gaze out at the harbor while you sip coffee and munch on a blueberry muffin or bacon and eggs. Hamburgers and sandwiches and wraps are on the lunch menu and the ice cream is great. They turn the grill off at 4:00 p.m. but you can get sandwiches until 5:00 p.m. The puzzle is how do you get up to Bumpa's since there is no visible entrance on Waterfront Highway. Steps are just around the west corner (walk a little way into Cardow's Walk). *No credit cards. 340.776.5674. Waterfront Hwy. at Cardow's Walk. BL $*

CAFE AMICI (3)
This stop in Riise's Alley offers a peaceful oasis away from the traffic. Umbrellas shade the little marble-top tables which are set on a long, narrow brick terrace. There's usually a soup, pasta, and sandwich of the day inscribed on the blackboard by the entrance and the menu includes sandwiches, salads,

73

and pastas. Good bets are the flank steak and blue cheese salad, sun-dried tomatoes and pine nuts over penne, grilled vegetables on a Kaiser roll, or a cheese steak on ciabatta bread. There are also several pizzas, including one with spinach, goat cheese, and sun-dried tomatoes and one with sausage, apples, mozzerella, and caramelized onions. *15% service is included in the bill. 340.776.5670. A.H. Riise Walkway. L $*

GLADYS' CAFE (6)

Gladys has owned several restaurants since she moved here from Antigua in 1969 and locals seek out her famous West Indian specialties, such as chicken soup with pigeon peas, pan-fried yellow tail with Creole sauce, curried chicken, and lemon-buttered conch. But she also prepares excellent hamburgers, salads, and meatloaf with mashed potatoes. Tired shoppers like to relax with one of Gladys' special soursop coladas. And morning shoppers stop here for a variety of omelets, French toast, and lox and bagels. *340.774.6604. Royal Dane Mall W.. BL $*

GREEN HOUSE (8)

This popular Waterfront Highway place is open to the breezes and busy all day long (and actually well into the evening). Come here for a late breakfast (they open at 10:30 a.m.) of huevos rancheros or eggs Benedict or a Creole omelet. Hamburgers, cheeseburgers, hot dogs, salads, a variety of sandwiches, and pizzas are served at lunch. *340.774.7998. Waterfront Hwy., west of Palm Passage at Stortvaer Gade, near First Bank. BLD $-$$*

HARD ROCK CAFE (11)

Booths and tables sit among rock 'n' roll decor at this typically-decorated Hard Rock Cafe. The moderate-priced menu features chili, cheese nachos, chef salad, California club (a BLT with a grilled marinated chicken breast and Swiss cheese), and their incredibly popular "Pig Sandwich" plus hamburgers and cheeseburgers, sundaes, banana splits, shakes and malts, and root beer floats. *340.777.5555. Waterfront Hwy. at International Plaza (upstairs). LD $-$$*

HERVE (1)

If you want a sophisticated setting, the comfort of air-conditioning, and a superb view of the harbor, walk up past the park across from the Post Office and then follow the stairs up to this excellent restaurant. The lunch menu features corn fritters, escargots, a delicious onion soup, many salads (including Caesar, chef, and roast duck), seafood crepes, quiche of the day, a tasty croque monsieur, and burgers. If you want to be outside, there is also a charming patio. *No lunch Sun. 340.777.9703. Government Hill. LD $-$$*

TAVERN ON THE WATERFRONT (5)

Tables line the windows at this air-conditioned, upstairs eatery overlooking the harbor. The lunch menu is simple, with burgers, soups, and salads. *Closed Sun. 340.776.4328. Waterfront Hwy. at Royal Dane Mall. LD $$*

VIRGILIO'S (9)

When you want an elegant lunch and some of the best Italian food anywhere, come here. Soft lighting and polished service provide the perfect backdrop for a glass of pinot grigio, a salad, and freshly grilled fish or the pasta of the day. Although Virgin Island power lunches are held here, Virgilio's is really meant for lingering and it's a fine place for a long and leisurely lunch. *340.776.4920. Main St. at Stortvaer Gade. LD $$-$$$*

SNACKS AND ICE CREAM

ICE CREAM SHOPPE (10)

This tiny take-away place has delicious ice cream cones, yogurt, and hot dogs, plus West Indian snacks like fish fry, johnnie cakes, chicken soup, and meat pates. *Tucked next to the Hard Rock Cafe souvenir store. $*

A SNACK IN THE PARK

If all the cruise ships are in town and the crowds are getting to you, or if you just feel like a snack and some space, you can always find a seat, some shade, and a bit of a breeze at Emancipation Park. And right across the street you'll find a street vendor or two where you can pick up anything from a cold bottle of water, to a snow cone, to all kinds of juices, to a bag of fresh-roasted peanuts, some chips, or a sugar cake. Whichever vendor you visit, they'll surely have a smile, something cold to drink, and a snack to take back to your seat in the park.

75

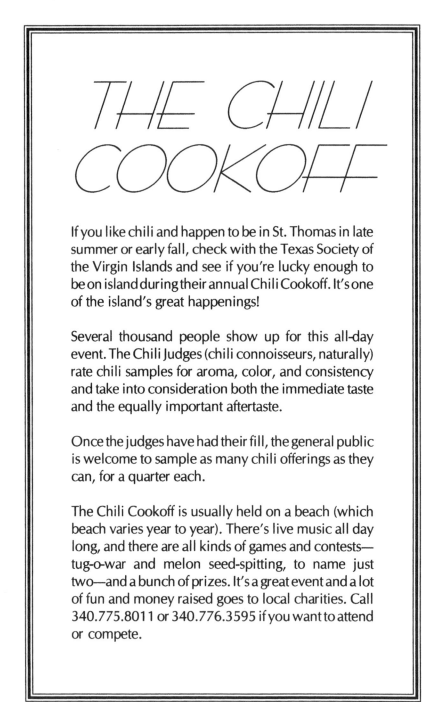

THE CHILI COOKOFF

If you like chili and happen to be in St. Thomas in late summer or early fall, check with the Texas Society of the Virgin Islands and see if you're lucky enough to be on island during their annual Chili Cookoff. It's one of the island's great happenings!

Several thousand people show up for this all-day event. The Chili Judges (chili connoisseurs, naturally) rate chili samples for aroma, color, and consistency and take into consideration both the immediate taste and the equally important aftertaste.

Once the judges have had their fill, the general public is welcome to sample as many chili offerings as they can, for a quarter each.

The Chili Cookoff is usually held on a beach (which beach varies year to year). There's live music all day long, and there are all kinds of games and contests—tug-o-war and melon seed-spitting, to name just two—and a bunch of prizes. It's a great event and a lot of fun and money raised goes to local charities. Call 340.775.8011 or 340.776.3595 if you want to attend or compete.

ST. JOHN FOR THE EVENING

Many visitors to St. Thomas never realize how incredibly easy it is to head over to St. John just for dinner. In fact, if you are staying on the east end of St. Thomas, it is possible to go to St. John for dinner in about the same length of time that it would take you to get to downtown Charlotte Amalie. Most of the ferries have an uncovered upper level and you can ride over basking in the afternoon sun and return at night in a seat open to the soft Caribbean breezes and under a blanket of stars and perhaps a full moon.

Getting to and from St. John
The ferry dock is right in the middle of the east end of St. Thomas, at Red Hook. Ferries run hourly on the half hour from 8 a.m. to midnight from Red Hook to Cruz Bay on St. John and the ride takes less than 20 minutes. Get there a little early if you want to be sure to get a seat up top. The fare is $3 and the ferry takes you to the dock right in the heart of Cruz Bay, which is St. John's only real town and very different from anything on St. Thomas. If you prefer a private ride, **Dohm Water Taxi** (*340.775.6501*) will take you over to St. John in one of their power catamarans in a quick 15 minutes and bring you back after dinner. It's $15 per person (minimum of six people) each way. *See page 111 for restaurants on St. John.*

Note: Ferries leave Cruz Bay on the top of the hour from 6 a.m. until 11 p.m. If you miss this last one, well...you're on St. John for the night.

A FULL DAY
IN PARADISE

A breakfast in bed or on a beach

A morning stroll and a swim

A few pages under the palms,
maybe a massage

A junket to St. John with lunch in Cruz Bay

A dessert or two by the dock

A soft drink for the voyage back

Another swim, a nap, a bubble bath

A cocktail under the stars

A romantic repast for two

A barefoot dance in the breezes

A port on the porch. . . and
then to bed.

CHAPTER 6

GREAT
ST. THOMAS
BEACHES
&
WATERSPORTS

"Babies don't need a vacation, but
I still see them at the beach."
—*Steven Wright*

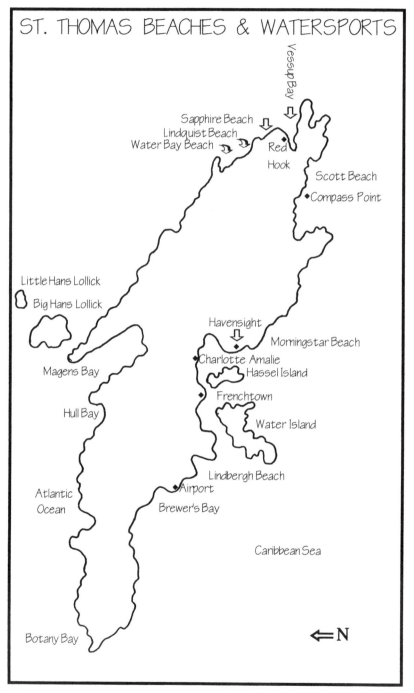

ST. THOMAS BEACHES & WATERSPORTS

Vessup Bay

Sapphire Beach
Lindquist Beach
Water Bay Beach
Red
Hook

Scott Beach
◆ Compass Point

Little Hans Lollick
Big Hans Lollick

Havensight
Morningstar Beach
◆ Charlotte Amalie
Hassel Island

Magens Bay

Frenchtown

Water Island

Hull Bay

Lindbergh Beach
◆ Airport
Atlantic
Ocean
Brewer's Bay

Caribbean Sea

Botany Bay

⇐ N

GREAT BEACHES

St. Thomas has many great beaches. Some are undeveloped. Others are in front of resorts. On St. Thomas, as in all of the USVI, all beaches are open to everyone, even if there's a resort there. Bear in mind that a beach in front of a resort is "groomed" at least once or twice a day. Workers pick up trash, rake the sand, and clip and water the tropical foliage that borders the beach. Anyone used to a "groomed" beach can think a natural beach in the Caribbean looks "messy," but it's not really. It's just that there's no one around to remove the seaweed, or pick up the detritus the waves have tossed onshore.

BOTANY BAY BEACH

It's way out at the western tip of the island, a very long drive and a bit of a walk, but the snorkeling is quite good here.

BREWER'S BAY BEACH

This beach is west of the airport (keep the airport on the left as you drive west on Brewer's Bay Drive—Rte 30, and then drive all the way through the campus of the University of the Virgin Islands.) This is a nice swimming beach and there are several snack trucks on weekends. This beach is close to the final approach to the St. Thomas airport and is a great place to see planes of all sizes.

HULL BAY BEACH

You'll see lots of little painted fishing boats bouncing at their buoys at this north shore beach. It's not a great swimming beach because there are so many little boats and it can be rough when the surf is up. There's a popular barefoot bar a bit behind the beach with weekend entertainment. The menu ranges from hot dogs to sandwiches to linguini with meat sauce.

LINDBERGH BEACH

Practically across the street from the airport, this nice long beach is great for walking and is also a calm swimming beach. Not very many large planes fly in and out of St. Thomas so the airport noise really isn't a problem. There are several hotels here, including the Island Beachcomber. You can rent jet skis and waverunners and go waterskiing here. There's also some fine food to be had at the little snack bar wagons parked along the road.

LINDQUIST BEACH

Also called Smith Bay Beach, it's on the eastern shore and it's one of the few easily-accessible beaches that is still completely undeveloped (although plans threaten to change this). The swimming here is excellent. This is a nice long beach lined with sea grapes. It's great for walking and taking in the views of Thatch Cay and Grass Cay. From Smith Bay Road (between the entrance to Pavilions and Pools and the Wyndham Sugar Bay) two dirt roads just yards from each other lead to this beach. One is about a minute north of Pavilions and Pools, is quite bumpy, and can involve encounters with big cows. The less bumpy, easier (no cows) dirt road is just a few yards further on and two signs make it easy to spot—coming from Red Hook, look for the green airport sign. If you're heading to Red Hook, turn left at the 35 mph sign.

MAGENS BAY BEACH
Year after year this long and stunning north shore beach is voted one of the world's ten most beautiful beaches, and it's both popular and easy to reach. It was donated to St. Thomas by Arthur S. Fairchild in 1946 to be preserved forever as a public park. The beach is a very long gentle curve of dazzling white sand and the water is exceptionally calm. There's a cafeteria-style snack bar and a large beach shop and you can rent beach chairs, floats, towels, snorkeling gear, and lockers. *$1 per vehicle and $3 per person entrance fee.*

MORNING STAR BEACH
Just outside of St. Thomas harbor, this beach is at Marriott Frenchman's Reef and Morning Star Resorts and there are several restaurants and bars along the beach. You can rent beach chairs, snorkel and windsurfing equipment, and take windsurfing and sunfish lessons. The beach is fairly long and generally calm for swimming, although it can have a swell with certain winds.

SAPPHIRE BEACH AND PELICAN BEACH
This half-mile-long beach fronts the Sapphire Beach Resort on the east end of St. Thomas. You can parasail from here, rent waverunners and sunfish, take windsurfing and scuba diving lessons, and rent floats and beach chairs. **Pelican Beach** is adjacent to the north and much quieter. Just scramble over the rocks.

SCOTT BEACH
You'll find this beach at the southeastern end of the island near Compass Point. You can rent beach lounges and umbrellas.

VESSUP BAY BEACH
This quiet beach is usually calm for swimming. It's near Cabrita Point.

WATER BAY BEACH
At the Renaissance Grand Beach Resort, this 1,000-foot-long beach is a good spot to rent jet skis, pedal boats, windsurfers, sunfish, and waverunners.

GREAT WATERSPORTS

St. Thomas offers practically every watersport imaginable. You can snorkel off the edge of a beach, take out a sunfish, go for a sail, scuba dive day or night, try your hand at parasailing, hop onto a jet ski or a waverunner, paddle a kayak, or pedal a pedal boat. You can also rent a little powerboat or charter a boat and visit beaches on other islands. St. Thomas is also a particularly good place to try one of these activities for the first time. Watersports centers here, more so than on most islands, really do specialize in teaching the beginner as well as outfitting the expert.

JET SKIS AND WAVERUNNERS

You can skim over the waves at many locations around the island of St. Thomas. Rent jet skis at **Marriott Frenchman's Reef Resort** (*340.776.8500*), at **Renaissance Grand Beach Resort** (*340.775.1510*), and at **Caribbean Fun** (*340.715.1030*) at Sapphire Beach Resort.

KAYAKING

In the Virgin Islands, there are actually two kinds of kayaking. Many resorts have brightly colored one- and two-person "kayaks" which are fun to take out and you can have races or just paddle about. The kayaking sport is also popular in the Virgin Islands. You can rent real kayaks and join kayaking trips. The waters off the east end of St. Thomas have many uninhabited islands and coves you can explore. Call **West Indies Wind Surfing** at Vessup Bay Beach (*340.775.6530; call first to make an appointment*). They rent kayaks and have kites that catch the wind and propel you—but don't let the wind take you too far in one direction or you'll have a long paddle back.

KAYAK AND SNORKEL TRIPS

Kayak into Mangrove Lagoon with naturalists from **Virgin Island Ecotours** (*340.779.2155*) and then snorkel and see juvenile reef fish, upside down jelly fish, barracuda, and rays. There's a wonderful full moon trip that includes dinner where the phosphorescence you stir up with your paddle almost outshines the moon and the stars.

PARASAILING

Want to take a ride 400 feet above the water? This popular sport is easy to do. You don't even have to get wet. You're strapped into a parachute, a speedboat surges forward, and up you go! Boats leave from many locations. Call **Caribbean Parasailing** (*340.775.9360*).

PEDAL BOATS

Quite a few St. Thomas resorts have these little contraptions. They look sort of silly but once you're in one, they can be fun. Basically two people sit in a floating set of chairs and pedal around—the faster you pedal, the faster you go. It's interesting to look back at the shore and a slow trip takes almost no energy. Bring a soda or a pina colada.

POWERBOATS

On calm days it can be wonderful fun to rent your own little powerboat and tool around in the water, or find a good snorkeling spot, or explore the uninhabited islands off the east end of St. Thomas. You can take a picnic to Lavango or Mingo Cay or even head over to a beach on St. John. If it's really calm and you feel like an adventure, you can also head to the BVI (bring a passport). **Nauti Nymph** (*340.775.5066*) in Red Hook offers 25', 29', and 31' boats with bimini tops, built-in ice coolers, swim ladders, VFH radios, charts, and safety gear. **Pocket Yachts** (*340.715.1015*) at Sapphire Marina rents 22' to 30' boats with similar features. Both companies rent snorkeling gear, too.

SCUBA DIVING

St. Thomas is surrounded by lots of good diving sites. If you've always wanted to try diving, now is a good time. It's possible to take a resort course and actually dive the same day. Call **Chris Sawyer Diving Center**, with locations at Red Hook (*340.777.7804*), the Renaissance Grand Beach (*340.715.6865, ext 7850*), or the Compass Point Marina (*340.775.7320*).

SNORKELING

Snorkeling equipment (mask, fins, snorkel) is available at virtually all resorts on St. Thomas and can be rented on many beaches. The water is clear here and you will see many colorful little fish. First-timers may want to try snorkeling right off the beach where it's sandy—although you won't see a lot of fish, it's still interesting to look around and you can practice breathing—slow and steady is the key. Once you can breathe easily, swim over to the rocky areas and see what is going on. If you want to go on a snorkeling trip (there are many to choose from) call the **Charterboat Center** (*340.775.7990*) and they'll match you with the trip that is right for you.

WINDSURFING

Lots of people spend hours trying to stay on these things. If you don't feel like trying it yourself, do find a good spot on the beach where you can watch someone else try. It's often very funny. Most resorts rent windsurfing equipment and also give lessons. If you want to windsurf and can't at your hotel then ask at reception which would be the closest place for you to go.

GOLF & TENNIS, FITNESS CENTERS, HORSEBACK RIDING

GOLF

George and Tom Fazio designed this championship 18-hole, 6022 yard, par 70 golf course at **Mahogany Run** *(800.253.7103 or 340.777.6006)* on the north side of the island.

The course is certainly one of the best-maintained courses in the Caribbean and the "Devils Triangle"—the 13th, 14th, and 15th holes—challenges the golfer to drive right over the Caribbean sea from atop a cliff.

TENNIS

There are some free public courts on the island, but whether you are looking for a lesson or just some court time, you are better off calling **Marriott Frenchman's Reef** *(340.776.8500)*, **Renaissance Grand Beach Resort** *(340.775.1510)*, and **Wyndham Sugar Bay** *(340.777.7100)* which all have courts available for a nominal fee to non-guests.

FITNESS CENTERS

When you feel the need for a workout, the following places have weight machines, free weights, treadmills, stairclimbers, bicycles, and even personal trainers.

Carib Health Complex at Sub Base *(340.777.1072)*

Gold's Gym (yes, just like in the states) next to the Hard Rock Cafe in Charlotte Amalie *(340.777.9474)*

SOME HELPFUL HINTS

DRIVING AROUND THE ISLAND

St. Thomas is an island of spectacularly steep hills and the views up top are simply stunning. It's definitely worth it to take a drive around the island. It's nice to have the freedom of a car, but consider taking a taxi tour first—to get your bearings, to get a sense of local driving habits and the steepness of the roads, and to be able to concentrate on the scenery instead of the curves.

WHAT, NO ELECTRICITY?

Don't worry when the electricity suddenly goes off. It happens all the time and it's no big deal. (That's why you have a candle in your hotel room.) You don't even have to be very patient as the power almost always comes right back on in just a few minutes. Don't worry. Be happy.

INVISIBLE BUGS WITH A BITE

At sundown, especially when it is not windy, annoying little 'no-see-ums' appear out of nowhere and bite. Insect repellant generally keeps them at bay and wind keeps them away. For some people, these bites have a lasting itch and it's good to have a medication like Sting-Eze around. A dab of gin will work in a pinch.

FERRY BOATS TO OTHER ISLANDS

Ferries to St. John and the British Virgin Islands leave from Red Hook and several spots along the waterfront at Charlotte Amalie. Ferries to St. Croix only leave from the Charlotte Amalie waterfront.

CHAPTER 7

GREAT ST. THOMAS ATTRACTIONS

"There are more than ninety-nine steps
to these ninety-nine steps."

—*Peter P., age 9*
from *Visiting the Virgin Islands with the Kids*

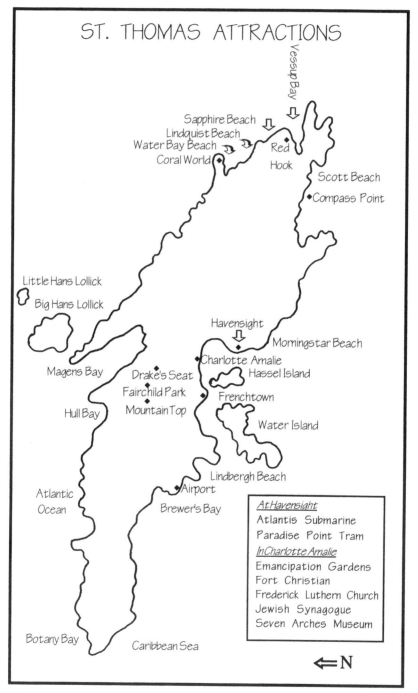

ST. THOMAS ATTRACTIONS

Vessup Bay

Sapphire Beach
Lindquist Beach
Water Bay Beach
Coral World
Red
Hook

Scott Beach
Compass Point

Little Hans Lollick
Big Hans Lollick

Havensight
Morningstar Beach
Charlotte Amalie
Hassel Island
Magens Bay
Drake's Seat
Fairchild Park
Frenchtown
Mountain Top
Hull Bay
Water Island

Lindbergh Beach
Atlantic
Ocean
Airport
Brewer's Bay

At Havensight
Atlantis Submarine
Paradise Point Tram
In Charlotte Amalie
Emancipation Gardens
Fort Christian
Frederick Luthern Church
Jewish Synagogue
Seven Arches Museum

Botany Bay
Caribbean Sea

⇐ N

HISTORICAL SIGHTS

There is much more to Charlotte Amalie than shopping. The town is listed in the National Register of Historic Places for its history and for its architecture. Below are descriptions of some of the most interesting buildings. If you want more information, you can find a nice selection of books and pamphlets (including an excellent walking tour) for sale in the Virgin Islands Museum shop at Fort Christian.

EMANCIPATION GARDEN

This is the park right in front of the Grand Galleria and is dedicated to the emancipation of the slaves in the Danish West Indies on July 3, 1848. Many local celebrations and events are held here. *Grand Galleria.*

FORT CHRISTIAN

You'll spot this red brick National Historic Landmark the first time you come to town. They've been restoring it for what seems like forever and there's still more to do. However, some good exhibits are open. It's the earliest known building in town and construction probably started around 1666. You can learn about famous local people, see examples of furniture that was typically in homes here 100 years ago, check out exhibits of shells, local fauna and flora, and birds. During the school year there are ever-changing exhibits by local students which focus on such things as protecting the environment and being kind to animals. *Donations welcome. 340.776.4566. Waterfront Hwy. Entrance around back.*

FREDERICK EVANGELICAL LUTHERAN CHURCH

This lovely church was established here in 1666 and the present building was started in 1789. A wide yellow brick stairway leads up to the arched entranceway. The ceiling of the church is dramatically arched and the wood in the chancel and pulpit is local mahogany. *Free. On Main Street, two blocks east of the Post Office.*

JEWISH SYNAGOGUE

Founded in 1796, this is the oldest Hebrew house of worship in continuous use under the U.S. flag. The benches and ark are fashioned out of local mahogany. The floor is sand, symbolic of a time when Jews in Spain were forced to practice their religion in secrecy and did so in cellars, using sand to muffle the sound. The walls here are made of bricks held together by sand, limestone, and molasses and it is said that years earlier children used to lick the walls to get a taste of the sweet molasses. *Donations accepted. Crystal Gade.*

89

SEVEN ARCHES MUSEUM

Ring the bell at the imposing black iron gate and someone will let you in to this restored private house, built with yellow ballast bricks from Denmark. Take a look at the stone oven in the original Danish kitchen. This is what people used to cook everything in, from stews and roasts to loaves of bread. Kids of all ages will like climbing up the steps to the high porch and seeing the many iguanas roaming about. *Small donation requested. 340.774.9295. Follow Main St. up over the hill east past the Government House and look for a little sign on the left. Follow the sign halfway down the alley.*

ATTRACTIONS AROUND THE ISLAND

St. Thomas has quite a number of "tourist attractions" but some of them really are quite special. Mountain Top and Drake's Seat are popular stops on the cruise ship crowd circuit, but you can see them without the throngs if you head to these sites in the early morning or late afternoon. Early, early morning is a great time to catch the views and take stunning photographs at scenic places that are always open, like Drake's Seat.

CORAL WORLD

The advertising can make this cluster of white geodesic domes look too "touristy" but what you see here is great and definitely worth a trip. So, what do you see? First of all, the **Underwater Observatory** lets you look right into a real reef. Circular stairs lead down into an underwater room ringed with windows that actually look right out into the ocean. You see the surface up above and all kinds of fish and underwater plants and corals, all in their natural habitat. It's like snorkeling without getting wet! You can spot live lobsters hiding in the rocks, shimmering silvery waves of giant schools of tiny fish moving as one, and fish hovering just outside the window, gawking at you. Don't get scared as you pass the **Predator Tank**, which is filled with fierce fish—sharks and barracudas. Then there are the **Marine Gardens**, a collection of individual aquariums showcasing sea life up close. Check out the incredibly delicate little seahorses, corals that glow in the dark, burrowing jawfish, and the moray eels. Kids of all ages get a kick out of patting a baby shark at the **Shark Shallows**, feeding stingrays at the **Stingray Pool**, and touching stuff in the "Touch Pond" which has all kinds of sea creatures including some weird ones—a sea cucumber that spits, a worm that goes inside itself when you touch it. The newest attraction is **Sea Trekkin'**—bring your bathing suit. It's for anyone over eight (and also over 80 pounds). You don a special Coral World

World helmet and roam the ocean floor in this guided undersea tour. Reservations are a must. By the way, if you hate crowds, go later in the day. You'll miss the talks and feedings but you'll be almost alone. *340.775.1555. $18 adult, $9 children 3-12, $58 family pass (2 adults and up to 4 children). Sea Trekkin' additional fee. Daily 9 a.m.–5 p.m. Coki Point.*

DRAKE'S SEAT

Legend has it that Sir Francis Drake used this place as a lookout to spot enemy Spanish fleets. It's now a parking area with a truly spectacular view of Magens Bay. Vendors selling T-shirts and such are here during cruise ship hours and there is a delightful donkey decked out in bougainvillaea blossoms that kids can have their picture taken with. Come here early morning or late afternoon to be alone and just absorb the stunning vista. *Route 40.*

FAIRCHILD PARK

A stone pathway and two benches offer spots for rest and relaxation and you can see both sides of the island at the same time from this very tiny, exquisitely peaceful park high up on a mountain. On a clear day, there's a spectacular, almost 360-degree view. *St. Peter Mountain Rd.*

MOUNTAIN TOP

Perched 1547 feet above sea level, this rather touristy attraction is one of the highest, easily accessible points on St. Thomas and a good choice for a stunning view overlooking St. Thomas and Magens Bay and the British Virgin Islands. There's a little restaurant, a number of shops, and a bar that specializes in daiquiris. Bring your camera. *Off of Route 33.*

PARADISE POINT TRAMWAY

Swiss-built gondolas carry you up 700 feet to the top of Flagg Hill and a spectacular view of Charlotte Amalie. The trip takes five minutes and stores and a restaurant and bar await you, a perfect place to relax and take in the view. *340.774.9809. Daily 9 a.m.-5 p.m. $12. Across from Havensight.*

SUBMARINE ATLANTIS

The journey begins with a 20-minute boat ride out to the air-conditioned 65' submarine. Once you board, it descends to 90 feet. Every seat looks out a 2' wide viewport and the scene is spectacular. Sea turtles, parrot fish, sergeant majors, queen angelfish, and yellow-tail snappers swim by. You'll see colorful corals and sponges. You are underwater for about 50 minutes, but the complete excursion takes two hours. *340.776.5650. $79 adults, $39 children (no children under 4). Trips daily Mon.-Sat. Call for schedules, which vary seasonally. Cruise ship dock at Havensight (building #6).*

CHARTERING A YACHT

Think about it. Whether you're an old salt who might want to captain your own boat or a fair weather sailor who wants a captain and crew, the steady winds, calm Virgin Island waters, and line of sight navigation make this the ideal place for a nautical vacation.

With wonderful, sheltered anchorages and the availability of just about any vessel you might imagine—from traditional sailboats to catamarans to sport fishers and trawlers and even motor sailors—you can't go wrong. A good place to find a charter is **Admiralty Yacht Vacations**. *P.O. Box 306162, St. Thomas 00803. Res: 800.544.0493 or 800.910.5228. Tel: 340.774.2172. Fax: 340.774.8010. www.admirals.com*

CATCHING THE BIG ONE

Chartering a yacht for a week is surely an adventure, but if you want to pack a whole bunch of on-the-sea excitement into one day, how about deep-sea fishing? Yes, a 1,282 pound blue marlin was caught in these waters awhile back, but the average here is a mere 200-300 pounds.

The boats are beautiful, the captains and crews are helpful, knowledgeable, and experienced and the excitement of the day can be an exhilarating and unforgettable event. Whether you're on St.. Thomas or St. John, you'll want the dynamic duo of Captain Bill McCauley and first mate Tyler Maltby of **Prowler Sportfishing Charters**. These two are rated the best of the best year after year. Whether you're an expert or beginner, want a half day or full, give them a call. *Red Hook, St. Thomas. 340.779.2515.*

THE INTERNET, E-MAIL, AND CYBER CAFES

These beautiful islands may seem like a million miles from "real life," but the truth is you're never very far from being "connected." Many hotels have data ports in the rooms and others have connected computers in the lobby that guests may use for a nominal charge. There are also a number of Cyber Cafes and communication centers with computers where you can go and log on.

ST. THOMAS

Beans, Bytes, and Websites (*340.776.7265, Royal Dane Mall, Charlotte Amalie*) is a great place to get connected. "Beans" refers to great coffees, espressos, and cappuccinos; "Bytes" to their great croissants, paninis, and desserts. And, well, "websites" means you can hook up, but they also offer a full line of services from faxing and scanning to computer services.

You can also log on at the upstairs internet facility at **Little Switzerland** (*340.776.2010, Main Street, Charlotte Amalie*).

St. Thomas Communications (*340.776.4324, 168 Crown Bay*) offers a full line of business services and computers and internet access, but without the food and drink.

ST. JOHN

Connections on St. John (*Cruz Bay, a block from the ferry dock, Tel: 340.776.6922; Coral Bay by Skinny Legs, Tel: 340.779.4994*) started out as a simple mail service over 20 years ago but has definitely "kept up with the times" and offers many services including Federal Express and Western Union, phones, faxes, internet access, and secretarial services.

Every Ting (*340.693.5820, south of Wharfside Village*) has a computer you can log onto (plus cappuccinos and more).

Quiet Mon (*340.779.4799, upstairs across from First Bank*) offers a great selections of beers and ales, or perhaps a fine Irish whiskey that one might sip while plugging into the net.

THE BRITISH VIRGIN ISLANDS FOR A DAY

One of the great things about staying on St. Thomas or St. John is that it is so incredibly easy to drop over to the British Virgin Islands for a day. It's hard to imagine how close these islands are to the USVI until you arrive and realize that you can practically swim to them. Though the BVI look very similar to the USVI— green and remarkably hilly—you'll find that in character, they are astonishingly different. You will definitely feel that you have visited another country—and perhaps even another era. You must have a valid passport to visit the BVI.

THE BVI FROM THE AIR
One of the quickest and most spectacular ways to get an overview of the BVI is to simply fly over them. Take off from the water in downtown Charlotte Amalie with **Seaborne Seaplane Adventures** (*340.773.6442*) for an exciting, 90-minute, narrated "flight-seeing" tour. The views are stunning.

THE BVI FROM THE WATER (GROUP TRIPS)
Powerboats are the only boats with enough speed to easily reach many British Virgin Islands in a day, so you get to see almost all the islands from the water, and you get to actually visit several islands. You are taken directly to excellent snorkeling areas and an expert goes in the water with you. From St. Thomas or St. John, **Limnos Charters** (*340.775.3203*) has 53' twin engine, smooth-riding catamarans and takes up to 40 people and **Stormy Petrel** and **Pirate's Penny** (*340.775.7990*) has 42' diesel single engine powerboats and takes up to 12 people. Both trips go along the north side of Tortola and on to the Virgin Gorda Baths and other islands for swimming and snorkeling.

THE BVI FROM THE WATER (PRIVATE CHARTER)
Go on **Rush Hour**, a high-speed 38' cigarette boat with 1000 hp, and at 70 mph, you can get all the way from Red Hook to The Baths on Virgin Gorda in about 45 minutes (that same trip, just one way, takes all day by sail!). Just call **High Performance Charters** (*340.777.7545*) to make arrangements. When you

want to customize a snorkeling or beaching or even a hiking trip to the BVI, call **Dohm Water Taxi** (*340.775.6501*). Their pilot/ guides are incredibly knowledgeable and can take you places and show you things most people don't know about—like the underwater lava flows off of Tortola. The **Charterboat Center** (*340.775.7990*; from the U.S. *800.866.5714*), located in Red Hook, specializes in trips to the British Virgin Islands and can arrange a variety of powerboat trips, sportfishing trips, day sails, and even weekly charters. If you're not sure what you want, they'll help you decide. Call ahead or stop by their offices.

RENTING YOUR OWN BOAT

This can be a great way to explore the beaches and snorkeling areas of the BVI. From St. Thomas you can reach Jost Van Dyke in 30 minutes, the Caves on Norman Island in 45 minutes, and The Baths on Virgin Gorda in 90 minutes. Everything is closer from St. John. Unless you're an old salt, don't even think of doing this on a really windy day. You'll be wet, scared to death, bounced about, and it will take forever to get anywhere. You must have a passport and clear customs (town dock on Jost Van Dyke, Yacht Harbour on Virgin Gorda, West End or Road Town in Tortola). *See page 84 to rent a boat on St. Thomas, page 128 for St. John.*

PUBLIC FERRIES TO THE BVI

It's a 30-minute trip from Red Hook, St. Thomas to West End, Tortola. From Charlotte Amalie, it's a 45-minute trip to West End and 90 minutes to Road Town, Tortola. Call **Native Son** (*340.774.8685*) or **Smith's Ferry** (*340.775.7292; they also have a trip to Virgin Gorda every other Saturday*). It's a 30-minute trip from Cruz Bay, St. John to West End, Tortola. Call **Inter-Island Ferry** (*340.776.6597*). On Fridays, Saturdays, and Sundays, Inter-Island ferries take passengers to the island of Jost Van Dyke from Red Hook, St. Thomas and Cruz Bay, St. John. You'll have time to explore, swim, and visit little beach bars, including Foxy's. Once a month, and twice when there is a blue moon, Inter-Island ferries leave early in the evening for Bomba's famous all-night Full Moon Parties on Tortola.

WHAT TO DO
ON ST. JOHN

St. John is a great place to be.
<u>What can you do there?</u>
You can hike on trails,
head to beautiful beaches,
follow the underwater snorkel trail
at Trunk Bay,
wander around the little town
of Cruz Bay,
browse through very original shops in one of the
prettiest shopping spots
in the Caribbean, Mongoose Junction,
look for a real mongoose,
rent a car and drive around the island
(take Centerline Road in at least one direction
to see spectacular views),
have an elegant brunch at Caneel,
have frozen drinks in funky bars,
take the Reef Bay Trail and see petroglyphs,
watch fabulous phosphorescence trails
on a night snorkel.

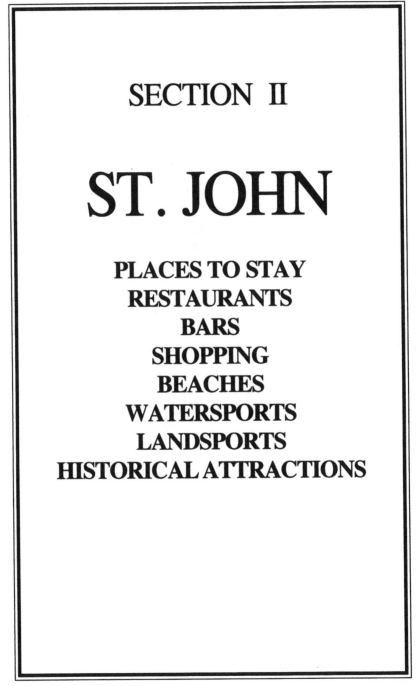

SECTION II

ST. JOHN

**PLACES TO STAY
RESTAURANTS
BARS
SHOPPING
BEACHES
WATERSPORTS
LANDSPORTS
HISTORICAL ATTRACTIONS**

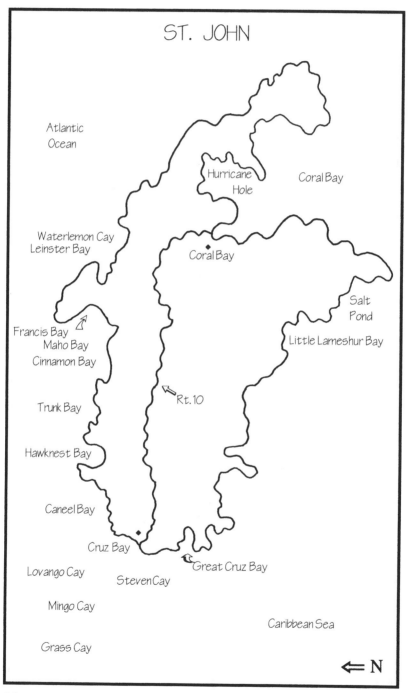

ST. JOHN

Atlantic Ocean

Hurricane Hole

Coral Bay

Waterlemon Cay
Leinster Bay

Coral Bay

Salt Pond

Francis Bay
Maho Bay
Cinnamon Bay

Little Lameshur Bay

Rt. 10

Trunk Bay

Hawknest Bay

Caneel Bay

Cruz Bay

Great Cruz Bay

Lovango Cay

Steven Cay

Mingo Cay

Caribbean Sea

Grass Cay

⇐ N

ABOUT ST. JOHN

St. John is a true one-of-a-kind destination and, in a way, has a bit of everything. The island is only 20 square miles and has a population of only 4,200, yet it entices an unusually wide assortment of visitors.

Two-thirds of St. John is part of the U.S. National Park system and the island is extraordinarily untouched. This is an island with terrific hiking trails, numerous exquisite beaches, and superb snorkeling. It's a wonderful place to explore and it's a real outdoor paradise. There are even great campgrounds. However, St. John is also home to a very U.S. mainland-style, full-service resort and to a sophisticated luxury retreat, both of which you never have to leave. There are also a few smaller lodging choices and there are villas to rent all over the island.

St. John is the place to come if you want to spend your days exploring the island by jeep, if you like to hike, if you want to lie on pristine beaches, or if you hope to find many wonderful snorkeling spots. It's a good island to come to if you wish to get away from crowds and do things on your own. St. John is much more isolated than St. Thomas. There's no airport here. You fly to St. Thomas and then take a ferry. Everything on St. John is on a much smaller scale than St. Thomas and it's a much, much quieter island.

St. John is also an island to come to if you want to stay at a luxury resort and be pampered. And it's a place to come if you want to go to little bars, dine outside on gourmet cuisine, or just want to munch a grilled cheese sandwich. You can be as casual or as formal as you want to be.

The "town" of Cruz Bay is about as tiny as you can get and still be a town, yet there are terrific original shops. Restaurants and bars are mostly casual, open-air, and small, yet you'll find very sophisticated cuisine here. The island is extremely hilly but main roads are well-maintained and the drives here are amazing. Roads run through forests and under canopies of trees. They climb alarmingly and drop precipitously, and there are some dicey hairpin curves, but the views and vistas are spectacular, switching back and forth from completely pristine steep green hills to shimmering sea and islands in the distance.

A SUGGESTED READING LIST

No assignments, just if you feel like it.

If you are a big reader, James A. Michener's
century-spanning tale, *Caribbean.*

For a humorous view of life in paradise,
Herman Wouk's *Don't Stop the Carnival.*

For those contemplating a life change, Sidney Hunt's
How to Retire in the Caribbean.

If you're going to Peter Island, Hugh Benjamin's
A Place Like This—and get Benji to autograph it.

If you're going to the BVI, Pam Acheson's
The Best of the British Virgin Islands, Third Edition.

For pirate lovers, Fritz Seyfarth's
Pirates of the Virgin Islands.

For interested readers, Mark Kurlansky's
A Continent of Islands
or Jamaica Kincaid's *A Small Place.*

If you are planning some serious exploring
in St. John, Pam Gaffin's
Feet, Fins, and Four-Wheel Drive.

Jimmy Buffett's bestseller, *A Pirate Looks at 50.*

If Jost Van Dyke is in your plans, Peter Farrell's
Foxy and Jost Van Dyke. Get Foxy to sign it.

CHAPTER 8

GREAT ST. JOHN PLACES TO STAY

"I never met a place like this
in my life."

—Hugh Benjamin
from *A Place Like This*

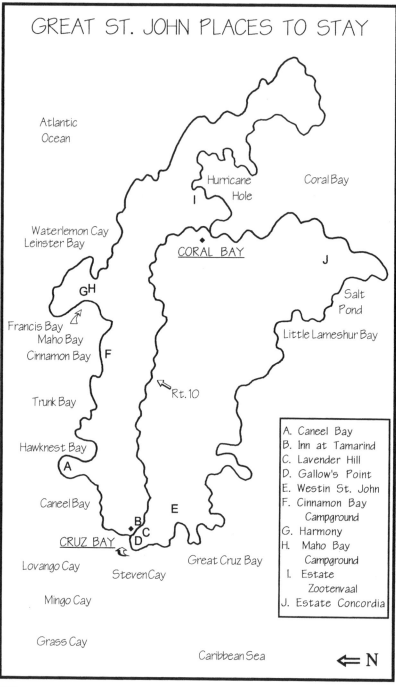

GREAT ST. JOHN PLACES TO STAY

Atlantic
Ocean

Hurricane
Hole

Coral Bay

I

Waterlemon Cay
Leinster Bay

CORAL BAY

J

G H

Salt
Pond

Francis Bay
Maho Bay
Cinnamon Bay

F

Little Lameshur Bay

Trunk Bay

Rt. 10

Hawknest Bay

A

Caneel Bay

E

B
C
D

CRUZ BAY

Lovango Cay

Steven Cay

Great Cruz Bay

Mingo Cay

Grass Cay

Caribbean Sea

N

A. Caneel Bay
B. Inn at Tamarind
C. Lavender Hill
D. Gallow's Point
E. Westin St. John
F. Cinnamon Bay
    Campground
G. Harmony
H. Maho Bay
    Campground
I. Estate
    Zootenvaal
J. Estate Concordia

GREAT ST. JOHN PLACES TO STAY

Over half of St. John is covered by the Virgin Islands National Park and much of the island is completely undeveloped. However, there are a number of wonderful lodging choices on the island and they run the gamut from full-service resorts all the way to campgrounds. You can stay near the little town of Cruz Bay or in the Virgin Islands National Park or in remote east end. In addition, scattered about all over the island are delightful houses for rent by the week or by the month.

Rates are per night without meals for two people on-season (off-season in parentheses) and do not include the additional 8% room tax or hotel service charges or special fees.

RENTING A HOUSE

People talk about renting villas in the Caribbean, but actually what you are getting most of the time is a house. St. John has a wonderful variety of rental houses to choose from. You can get just about any kind, from a very modest house with simple furnishings and no view and no pool (which is just fine if you plan to spend your days exploring the beaches around the island) to an elegantly furnished four-bedroom villa with a large pool, stunning views, and maid and chef service. You will need to rent a car for your stay, unless you plan to get groceries on the way in and never leave.

Rental houses are either on or above a beach, on the water and near a beach, or up in the hills. Although beachfront houses make it delightfully easy to go to the beach, remember that they are generally less private, simply because the beaches are public. Rental houses in the hills can have stunning views, and the higher up you go, the more breathtaking the scene, but bear in mind that St. John is incredibly hilly and roads are very steep. Before you rent, look at a map of St. John and decide what you'd like to be near, such as Cruz Bay or the north shore beaches or Coral Bay. Houses are rented by the week, and rates run all the way from $1,500 to $10,000.

Caribbean Villas & Resorts*, P.O. Box 458, Cruz Bay, 00831. Res: 800.338.0987. Tel: 340.776.6152. Fax: 340.779.4044. www.caribbeanvilla.com*

Catered To*, Marketplace Suite 206, Cruz Bay, 00831. Res: 800.424.6641. Tel: 340.776.6641. Fax: 340.693.8191. www.cateredto.com*

Destination St. John*, P.O. Box 8306, Cruz Bay, 00830. Res: 800.562.1901. Tel: 340.779.4647. Fax: 340.715.0073. www.destinationstjohn.com*

McLaughlin Anderson Luxury Villas*, 1000 Blackbeard's Hill, St. Thomas, 00802. Res: 800.537.6246. Tel: 340.776.0635. Fax: 340.777.4737. www.mclaughlinanderson.com*

CANEEL BAY

If you want understated luxury, and to combine hours of relaxing on very private beaches with exceptional service and elegant cuisine, you can't beat this longtime favorite.

Caneel Bay is on a 170-acre, vaguely hilly peninsula rimmed with seven stunning white sand beaches that are exceptionally private, because most of the property is accessible only to guests. The scenery here is spectacular. Peaceful paths lead to hammocks, benches, and quiet beaches across wide expanses of manicured green lawn radiant with blossoming hibiscus and bougainvillaea. From almost anywhere, you can see shades of azure Caribbean waters dotted with hilly, distant islands. Despite the fact that there are 166 units, beaches and paths can be remarkably empty.

Most rooms are in one- and two-story buildings that are beachfront but tucked discretely behind sea grape trees. Others are waterfront or near the tennis courts. Rooms are inviting, expensively but casually decorated, and very comfortable. Some have stonework walls and spacious showers and all have air-conditioning, mini-bars, safes, coffee makers, irons, and robes. Children are welcome at Caneel Bay but two beaches (Scott and Paradise) are designated as "quiet beaches for those wishing to hear only the quiet lapping of the waves" and these beaches are off-limits to children under 13. The rooms behind these two beaches are one-story and designated as "premium" and have patios that look through the sea grapes to the beach. Meals are a pleasure at all of the restaurants and the cuisine is superb. Turtle Bay Estate, which is only open to resort guests, is especially elegant, even at breakfast.

Don't come here if you want a lot of action or or if you want a TV or phone (much less computer ports) in your room or opulent jacuzzi bathrooms. Caneel's luxury and elegance is subtle. You'll find it in the fine stonework arches, or the way the beachfront rooms have splendid water views yet are hidden in the sea grapes, so as not to spoil the untouched feel of the beach. This is one of the few luxury resorts left where you can actually leave the real world behind. Guests young and old come back year after year because, for them, this kind of escape is one of the most relaxing and restorative experiences there is.

4 restaurants, bar, pool, 11 tennis courts, 7 beaches (excellent snorkeling), massage, fitness center, hiking, shop, cell phones on request, office center. Airport check-in and private ferry ($65 and includes unlimited trips to St. Thomas). Rates: $450-$875 ($300-$575). Special packages. 166 units. P.O. Box 720, Cruz Bay, 00831. Res: 800.928.8889. Tel: 340.776.6111. Fax: 340.693.8280. www.rosewood-hotels.com

GALLOWS POINT SUITE RESORT

*Stay here for spectacular views and superb snorkeling right out front.
Cruz Bay is just a short walk away.*

The land that wraps around the southern end of Cruz Bay ends with a
promontory known as Gallows Point. Fourteen grey, two-story, quadraplex
condominiums are clustered here. From the water they appear almost too close
to each other, but from the inside, tall, louvered doors completely fold back
and showcase sensational views of turquoise waters and nearby islands and you
completely forget that anyone could be right next door. All units have a
separate bedroom, fully-equipped kitchen, a living/dining area with a sleeper
sofa, ceiling fans, TV/VCR, and patio or balcony. All units are air-conditioned.
Second-floor units are more spacious and have high ceilings over the living
areas, loft bedrooms with a half-bath, and more dramatic views. All units have
tile floors and are furnished in rattan and tropical prints. The pool and beach
are quite tiny but the snorkeling is really superb all along the shore heading
away from Cruz Bay. ZoZo's (*see page 115*), the on-site restaurant, is one of
the finest on the island and its third floor bar is one of the best places on St.
John to watch the sun set and to try and catch the green flash.
*Restaurant, bar, small pool, tiny beach, shop, activities center. 60 units. Rates:
$365-$465 ($200-$265). P.O. Box 58, Cruz Bay, 00831. Res: 800.323.7229.
Tel: 340.776.6434. Fax: 340.776.6520. www.gallowspointresort.com (11
units available through www.gallowspoint.com)*

LAVENDER HILL SUITES

*This small condominium complex offers comfortable apartment living
with a pool, and you can walk to town.*

Apartments are in two buildings that peek out from the top of tropical foliage
on a hillside overlooking Cruz Bay. There are eight one-bedroom apartments
and four two-bedroom penthouse apartments. All units have a separate
bedroom, a living-dining area, a fully-equipped kitchen, and a TV/VCR. Units
also have air-conditioning and ceiling fans. Each condominium is privately
owned and decor varies, but generally you can count on tile floors, rattan
furniture, and pastel prints. Long, wrap-around balconies catch the tropical
breezes and are perfect spots to read or just gaze at the view and watch the
harbor traffic in the distance. A nice size pool is nestled in between the two
buildings. Cruz Bay restaurants and shops are just a short walk down the hill.
*Pool. 12 units. Rates: $325-$495 ($175-$275). P.O. 567, Cruz Bay, 00831.
Res: 800.348.8444 or 800.975.5001. Tel: 340.776.6969. Fax: 340.779.4486.
www.lavenderhill.net*

HARMONY STUDIOS

Kids and grown-ups alike get a kick out of this place, which is built entirely out of recycled materials.

Nestled among the trees above Maho Bay are these delightfully contemporary, comfortable duplex units built entirely out of recycled materials. You'd never guess what everything once was, even if you look very closely! Just for starters, the roof is made out of recycled cardboard, the doormat was fashioned out of melted old tires, the shiny walls were once newspapers, the shower tiles are created out of crushed light bulbs, and the outdoor furniture was originally soda bottles! Even some of the decor was once something else, like the throw rugs woven from plastic milk bottles. Don't be frightened. Nothing even vaguely resembles what it once was and these units are very comfortable and attractive. Studios come in two sizes. In either size, upstairs units have better views, more of a breeze, and cathedral ceilings. All have kitchenettes (low-voltage refrigerator, of course) and spacious decks, and spectacular views. There's a beautiful beach down the hill. This is one of ecologist Stanley Selengut's marvelous brainstorms.

12 units. Rates: $195-$220 ($110-$145). P.O. Box 310, Cruz Bay, 00831. Res: 800.392.9004. Tel: 340.776.6240. Fax: 340.776.6504. www.maho.org

THE INN AT TAMARIND COURT

This simple 20-room "bed and breakfast" has its own popular restaurant and is conveniently just a few steps outside of Cruz Bay.

As you walk past the Caribbean pastel-colored sign into the courtyard and see the little fountain, the delightful bar, and the umbrella-shaded tables and chairs, you begin to sense you are in the midst of "Caribbean casual." This recently refurbished "in town" inn has 20 rooms, all with air-conditioning, cable television, small refrigerators, and daily maid service. The inn offers two suites for up to four guests, standard rooms for one or two, and economy singles that share a bath. (Very European.) The on-site restaurant serves breakfast daily and has a different island chef and theme for dinner each night, from Italian to sushi to barbecue. The bar area is also a favorite gathering place for locals and tourists alike. The recent renovations and improvements, the caring on-site management, the sensible prices, and the location make this a popular choice for those happy with fairly basic accommodations. A swimming pool is in the works.

Bar, restaurant. 20 units. Rates: $75-$240 ($60-$160). General Manager: Barry Evans. P.O. Box 350, Cruz Bay, 00831. Res: 800.221.1637. Tel: 340.776.6378. Fax: 340.776.6722. www.tamarindcourt.com

WESTIN ST. JOHN RESORT & VILLAS

Busy and bustling, this full-service resort is the most stateside-like lodging on St. John and both honeymooners and families flock here.

This resort is set on 47 acres that sweep down to a long crescent of white sand and look out to a harbor of sailboats gently rocking at anchor. Colorful two-story buildings cascade down to the beach, separated by strips of green lawn, rows of palm trees, well-tended beds of brilliant tropical flowers, and broad brick walkways. Rooms are spacious and contemporary. Walls are painted in soft colors with deeper hued woodwork and doors, and prints hang on the walls. All rooms have signature Westin "Heavenly" beds and showers plus mini-bars, TV and in-room movies, large bathrooms, safes, coffee makers, robes, and irons. The closer you are to the beach, the better the water view.

Upstairs in the main reception building and open to the breezes is the light and airy Chloe & Bernard's, the resort's fancy dinner restaurant. Down the hill and facing the beach is the Beach Cafe & Bar, which is open for breakfast, lunch, and dinner plus a lavish Sunday brunch. There's a very casual lunch and snack stop near the pool, and a bar right next to the pool. There's also a complete deli where you can buy sandwiches, cookies, a small selection of groceries, and daily specials. Room service is offered round-the-clock, including pizza to munch on while you watch one of the current in-room movies.

Activities center around the 1,200-foot beach and the quarter-acre, geometric-shaped pool, complete with two jacuzzis and a small waterfall. The watersports center offers windsurfing, snorkeling, jet skiing, parasailing, plus fishing, sailing, and scuba trips. A car rental company is on the property.

The beach and the pool keep children busy but there is also an outstanding Kids Club which offers children ages three to 12 a full range of indoor and outdoor activities. It's open for half-day, full-day, and evening sessions and kids learn island arts and crafts, find out all about iguanas, and get involved in beach activities and volleyball games. On the far side of the entrance, nestled among trees and dense foliage, are 67 vacation villas available for rent or for vacation ownership. Some have private pools.

3 restaurants, 3 bars, pool, beach, 6 tennis courts, fitness center, spa, 2 shops, deli. Airport check-in and private ferry ($65 per person, $45 ages 4-12; includes unlimited trips to St. Thomas). 285 units. Rates: $539-$669 ($159-$339) plus $15 per night resort charge. Special packages. P.O. Box 8310, Cruz Bay, 00831. Res: 888.627.7206. Tel: 340.693.8000. Fax: 340.779.4500. www.westinresortstjohn.com

107

EAST END LODGING

The east end of St. John is about a 20-minute very hilly drive from Cruz Bay and extremely isolated. Spread along the shore are a few ultra-casual restaurants, a deli of sorts, a little grocery, and some shops.

ESTATE CONCORDIA STUDIOS & ECO-TENTS

These two adjacent properties are award-winning examples of ecologically sensitive developments.

Ten bumpy minutes past Coral Bay (and a good 45 minutes from Cruz Bay) you'll come to environmentalist Stanley Selengut's latest creations. Nine studios and two-story duplexes and 11 eco-tents are tucked into the hillside in this very remote part of St. John. Units have a variety of configurations but all have full or partial ocean views and efficiency or full kitchens. The eco-tents have comforts that bring staying here a big notch above regular camping.
Pool. 9 studios and duplexes, 11 eco-tents. Rates for studios: $135-$200 ($95-$150). Rates for eco-tents: $125 ($85). P.O. Box 310, Cruz Bay, 00831. Res: 800.392.9004. Tel: 340.776.6226. Fax: 340.776.6504. www.maho.org

ESTATE ZOOTENVAAL

These simple cottages are the place to come when you want a peaceful, remote, "no frills" type of getaway and great snorkeling.

Three whitewashed bungalows are set along a low hill across the road from the water, each with a patio and spacious yard. Interiors are basic but very clean and extremely well-kept. Well-placed louvres bring in the sea breezes and keep the cottages cool (and you can sleep to the sound of the lapping waves). Cook a gourmet meal in the full kitchen or stick to the simple life here. It's your choice. (You'll need to stock up on food and supplies in St. Thomas or on St. John at the Star Market just above Cruz Bay, which is expensive but carries most everything and even has a butcher, or bring supplies with you from the states). Across the street stairs lead down to a little, somewhat rocky beach on Hurricane Hole Bay. Estate Zootenvaal and the bay are within the Virgin Islands National Park boundaries and no boats are allowed to anchor in the bay which means the waters are undisturbed and the snorkeling is superb. Coral Bay establishments are just a few minutes away.
3 units. Maid service extra. Weekly rates for two people: one bedroom $1,750 (extra person $525), two bedroom $2,310 (each extra person $630). Daily rates available. General Manager: Robin Clair. Hurricane Hole, 00830. Tel: 340.776.6321. www.usviguide.com/zootenvaal

CAMPGROUNDS
CINNAMON BAY CAMPGROUND
Here, rustic cottages, tents, and bare sites are hidden in the trees just minutes from a gorgeous white sand beach.

Cinnamon Bay, which is in the Virgin Islands National Park, is St. John's longest beach. Set back against the hills and concealed among the tropical foliage, is this superb campground. There are three types of accommodations, all within a two-minute walk from the beach and all with picnic table and charcoal grill. You have the choice of screen-lined, 15' by 15' "cottages," with electric lights, ceiling fan, four twin beds and linens (changed twice weekly), propane gas stove, ice chest, cooking and eating utensils; canvas 10' by 14' tents on a solid floor, with a gas lantern, cots, linens (changed twice weekly), propane gas stove, ice chest, cooking and eating utensils; and bare sites, which can handle one large tent or two smaller tents. Bathrooms are nearby and there are public phones, a message center, safe deposit boxes, and lockers. Breakfast and lunch are served at a snack bar and the open-air restaurant Tree Lizards dishes up seafood, barbecues, and vegetarian delights every evening and even West Indian music on-season. The Beach Shop and Activities Deck arranges snorkeling, windsurfing, sea kayaking, and sailboat rentals, plus sailing cruises and scuba and snorkeling trips. Winter months fill up as far as a year in advance.

Restaurant, snack bar, beach, grocery store, gift shop. 126 units. Rates: cottages $110-$145 ($70-$90), tents $80 ($58), bare sites $27. P.O. Box 720, Cruz Bay, 00831. Res: 800.539.9998. Tel: 340.776.6330. Fax: 340.776.6458. www.cinnamonbay.com

MAHO BAY CAMPGROUND
Come here for hillside camping on a small but beautiful beach.

Fourteen acres of seemingly pristine forested hillside rise up from a classic, white sand beach, yet here and there, clusters of open-sided, 16' by 16' tent cottages exist among the trees. It's amazing how very undisturbed the land is. Stairs and elevated walkways wind around trunks, interrupting nothing. Opened in the early '70s, this was Stanley Selengut's first ecological venture on St. John and it is still going strong. Beds, tables, chairs, propane stoves, and cooking utensils are provided. Some tents have superb water views. There's an outdoor restaurant for breakfast and dinner and an activities desk offers sailing, snorkeling, windsurfing, and other watersports.

Restaurant. 114 units. Rates: $115 ($75). P.O. Box 310, Cruz Bay, 00831. Res: 800.392.9004. Tel: 340.693.6596. Fax: 340.776.6504. www.maho.org

HISTORICAL ATTRACTIONS ON ST. JOHN

ANNABERG SUGAR MILL

This sugar mill operated well into the late 1800s and these ruins are well-preserved and a delight to visit. The National Park brochure identifies the buildings, describes how sugar was produced, and even names fruit trees. The view of the British Virgin Islands from here is superb. Periodically there are historical reenactments and island baking and cooking demonstrations. *340.776.6201. Rt. 20, near Leinster Bay.*

ELAINE IONE SPRAUVE LIBRARY & MUSEUM

Built in 1757, this former Great House is now a library and a museum, with a small collection of Indian pottery and artifacts from ancient and colonial days. There are permanent exhibits on Danish West Indian history, natural history, and arts and crafts. Come here also to see ever-changing exhibits of work by local artists. *Open weekdays 9-5. 340.776.6359. Cruz Bay.*

IVAN JADAN MUSEUM

Ivan Jadan, considered one of the greatest Russian tenors of all time, spent his last 40 years on St. John. He died in 1995 and his wife has lovingly created this museum, a tribute to the classical singer's 92-year life and love for music. Historic photos, documents, and items are on display and there are numerous books you are welcome to read and you can listen to some of his performances, too, including the posthumously-released CD, "Songs of the Heart." *Mon.-Sat. 9-11, 4-6, and by appointment. 340.776.6423. Genip St., Cruz Bay.*

CHAPTER 9

GREAT ST. JOHN RESTAURANTS & BARS

"Only Irish coffee provides in a single glass
all four essential food groups:
alcohol, caffeine, sugar, and fat."

—Anonymous

GREAT ST. JOHN RESTAURANTS & BARS

Atlantic
Ocean

Hurricane
Hole

Coral Bay

CORAL BAY

Waterlemon Cay
Leinster Bay

Salt
Pond

Francis Bay
Maho Bay
Cinnamon Bay

C

Little Lameshur Bay

Rt. 10

Trunk Bay

Hawknest Bay

A

A. Caneel Bay
   Terrace and
   Equator
B. Asolare
C. Chateau
   Bordeaux
D. Chloe & Bernard
All other
restaurants
and bars in this
chapter are in Cruz
Bay or Coral Bay.

Caneel Bay

B

D

CRUZ BAY

Lovango Cay

Steven Cay

Mingo Cay

Caribbean Sea

Grass Cay

⇐ N

GREAT ST. JOHN RESTAURANTS & BARS

One of the most magical and enchanting features of the Caribbean is the ability to have elegant meals on terraces that are open to the outdoors, to combine a sophisticated and refined style of dining with soft breezes and romantic nighttime scenery—sparkling stars, rising moons, twinkling distant lights.

While St. Thomas restaurants often are indoors and professionally decorated, even the finest St. John restaurants rely on the outdoor scenery and island breezes to create an inviting background for an elegant meal. In fact, it is possible to walk by an excellent restaurant on St. John in the afternoon and see only a stack of chairs on a concrete floor, and a padlock and chain draped around the kitchen door. You just know that place must be closed for good. Yet return in the evening, and you'll find tablecloths, candlelight, and glistening wine buckets.

Cruz Bay restaurants and bars, which are described first in this chapter, are all within walking distance of each other. Coral Bay restaurants and bars are described on page 119. Bear in mind that, off-season, hours and days of operation may vary and it is wise to call ahead. On-season, it's a good idea to make a dinner reservation at the fancier restaurants.

ST. JOHN'S FINEST RESTAURANTS

ASOLARE

The modest lattice and stonework entrance belies the stunning scenery that awaits you once inside. This small, elegant restaurant is set high up on a hillside in a restored stone house and the entire front looks out to a spectacular panorama of azure waters and distant islands. At night, the twinkling lights of St. Thomas are magical. The view alone would be worth the visit, but you'll find that the exquisitely-presented, contemporary Asian cuisine is equally outstanding. You might start with a shiitake and grilled oyster mushroom tower wrapped in spring roll sheets with a hoisin glaze, Asian micro-ginger beef kabobs, or barbecued shrimp with grilled baby eggplants and zucchini. Good dinner choices include a crown roast of lamb on black tea couscous, sesame-crusted tuna, pan-seared sea bass and seaweed risotto, a caramelized veal chop, or Thai shrimp and scallop curry. *340.779.4747. A two-minute cab ride from Cruz Bay on Caneel Hill. D $$-$$$*

113

CANEEL BAY TERRACE

For elegant buffets with outstanding selections—for lunch, dinner, and even breakfast—you can't beat the Caneel Bay Terrace at Caneel Bay resort. The buffets here are among the very best anywhere and quite reasonably priced (for example, $25 for the lunch buffet, $22 for cold selections only).The cuisine is of the finest quality, the al fresco setting is peaceful, and the service gracious and refined. Well-spaced tables look out to a bay and there are numerous hot and cold selections plus cooked-to-order choices, all beautifully presented. *Buffets are breakfast and lunch Mon.-Sat., brunch Sun., dinner Mon. (Grand Buffet) and Wed. or Fri. Reservations for dinner essential (inquire about dress code). 340.776.6111. On Rte. 20, five minutes north of Cruz Bay. BLD $$*

CHATEAU BORDEAUX

This is just about the highest place you can drive to on St. John and the attentive service and gourmet cuisine at this restaurant are a perfect match for the breathtaking, airplane-like views. Try to get here before dark so you can see the stunning colors at sunset time and the truly amazing vista of the British Virgin Islands. Appetizers include a caramelized onion, swiss chard, and goat cheese tart; a duck and chanterelle ravioli; and a grilled calamari salad. For entrees, the roasted pork loin with endive and sweet potato gnocchi or the Caribbean bouillabaisse or porcini-dusted mahi are excellent choices. Driving here in the dark is not for the faint of heart, so consider taking a cab unless you know the road. Lunch is served on the outside deck only and the simple menu includes cheeseburgers and daiquiris. *Reservations for dinner essential. 340.776.6611. Centerline Rd. at Carolina Hill. LD $$-$$$*

CHLOE & BERNARD'S

The decor is exotic at this independently run restaurant at the Westin St. John. Gauzy fabric panels cascade down from the cathedral ceiling and tables are nestled in dimly-lit alcoves between giant white pillars. The cuisine is multinational, including French, Swiss, Italian, Cuban, and Tasmanian offerings. Black mussels with ginger and a coconut rum cream sauce, shrimp bisque with French cognac, and ceviche Havana style are some of the starters. Main courses include steamed red snapper with smoked oysters and fresh ginger, sauteed shrimp with almonds over angel hair pasta, and tenderloin of beef with green, red, and white peppercorn cream sauce. *Entertainment three nights a week. Reservations essential. 340.714.6075. Five minutes west of Cruz Bay. D $$$*

EQUATOR

Stone steps wind up through bougainvillaea to the open-air dining level of this restored sugar mill at Caneel Bay resort. It's dark and romantic and some nights a soft steel pan duo entertains. The eclectic menu features Caribbean and Asian dishes as well as great steaks. You might begin with a lobster bisque or jerk-seared tuna or a spinach and arugula salad. Entrees include broiled mahi with creole pilaf, seared ahi tuna with pumpkin sweet potato corn hash, Caribbean lobster, and N.Y. strips, T-bones, and filets. Save room for the brownie with pistachio ice cream or the white chocolate pudding. *Closed Sun. Reservations essential. 340.776.6111. On Rte. 20, five minutes north of Cruz Bay. D $$$*

PARADISO

Stonework walls and French doors mark the entrance to this large and appealing restaurant. Inside, high ceilings, pastel walls, framed art, tropical plants, and hardwood floors create a sophisticated and upscale background for fine cuisine. Pan-seared day boat scallops, sauteed rock lobster medallions, and a lightly warmed spinach salad are good choices for starters. Then try the pan-roasted local wahoo or swordfish, oven-roasted double cut pork chops with golden barley wild rice risotto, pan-seared local tuna with wild spinach and baby mushrooms, or free range chicken with roasted vegetables. On cool nights, the brick balcony, lined mostly with tables for two, is a romantic choice. *340.693.8899. Mongoose Junction. D $$-$$$*

STONE TERRACE

Broad steps lead up a rather grand stonework entrance to this pleasant al fresco restaurant with nicely spaced tables and arched wooden doors. Tables are set on a terrace and look out to the harbor. The ambitious and appealing menu includes Caribbean conch chowder with applewood smoked bacon, Thai curry chicken spring roll, oysters Rockefeller, and seared tuna sashimi on spinach salad for starters. For main courses, the rack of lamb with a crispy Dijon onion crust, molasses-rubbed pork tenderloin, black peppercorn-encrusted tuna, or the lobster preparation of the day are all good choices. *Closed Mon. 340.693.9370. Just south of Wharfside Village. D $$-$$$*

ZOZO'S RISTORANTE

When you want to have an outstanding dinner in an exceptionally beautiful setting, head to this elegant northern Italian al fresco restaurant. White table linens, candles, a lovely view of neighboring islands, and tropical breezes provide the perfect backdrop for an exquisite meal. Start with the beef carpaccio, or the grilled diver scallops on warm tuscan beans, or the baby spinach and mushroom salad with goat cheese vinaigrette or share an antipasto for two. Then move on to the shrimp over linguini with shiitake mushrooms or the osso bucco or the pan-seared tuna wrapped in prosciutto on saffron risotto. Be sure to arrive early for a drink at the upstairs bar with absolutely stunning sunset views. *Reservations essential on-season for this very popular restaurant. 340.693.9200. Gallow's Point Resort. D $$-$$$*

115

CASUAL CRUZ BAY FAVORITES

BANANA DECK

Wooden stairs lead up to this ultra-casual eatery tucked into the hillside between banana tree groves and overlooking the waters of Cruz Bay. There's a wide outdoor dining deck with simple tables and an occasional umbrella. Up one more level is a long bar and one can eat here, too. This is the place to come for cheeseburgers and fries, a cheese and chili hot dog, or conch fritters. *340.693.5055. Across from south end of Wharfside Village. LD $-$$*

CHILI BILLY'S

This snug, upstairs, open-air, and extremely casual hillside spot serves hamburgers, cheeseburgers, large salads, soups, and sandwiches, including an excellent club. Scrambled eggs, omelets, Monkeybread French toast, and other breakfast items are available until closing. If the deck is full, have a seat at the small indoor counter. *340.693.8708. Across from the lumberyard. BL $*

FISH TRAP

Locals and visitors keep this popular restaurant full year-round. Tables are in several open-air rooms and on balconies and there's never an empty one. Fish lovers have a hard time choosing between the five or six "catches of the day" and shrimp, scallops, or lobster. Seafood choices are also paired with steaks, and there are several pasta dishes, including a vegetarian primavera. The conch fritters and Fish Trap chowder both make fine appetizers. *Closed Mon. 340.693.9994. Near south end of Wharfside Village. D $$*

LA TAPA

Stucco walls, arched doorways, and roughly-hewn, dark wooden tables create a decidedly Spanish atmosphere at this cozy and very popular eatery. The menu changes somewhat from night to night but usually includes such soups as a green curry potato bisque and a spicy gazpacho. Appetizers and salads range from a shrimp brochette or seared fois gras with apple duck glace to a sumptuous cashew-encrusted goat cheese. Excellent entree choices are the seared tuna with passion fruit soy glaze, the grilled beef filet with truffled morel sauce, or the paella for two. Additional tables are outside, but some find the traffic a bit noisy. There's jazz here some evenings. *340.693.7755. Across from First Bank. D $$*

LIME INN

Plants hang from the ceiling and decorate the latticework at this casual, open-air, and incredibly popular spot tucked in the back of an esplanade. Crowds come here nightly for grilled fish, N.Y. strip, and Caribbean lobster. Wednesday night is the extremely well-attended, all-you-can-eat Shrimp Feast (no reservations). Quiches, soups, salads, burgers, and sandwiches are available at lunch. *No lunch Sat. Brunch only Sun. 340.779.4199. Lemon Tree Mall. LD $$*

MARGARITA PHIL'S

For really outstanding authentic Mexican food in a casual setting, you can't beat Margarita Phil's. The setting is cozy and very informal, with a little indoor bar, several indoor tables, and a little outdoor patio. Phil, the chef and owner, spends his vacation time in Mexico every year, learning new recipes and cooking techniques. A dedicated chef, he's in the kitchen every day, preparing outstanding Mexican delights. Enchiladas, tacos, fajitas, chalupas, quesadillas—you can't go wrong here. The sides (like the beans and rice) are outstanding, too. Also try the salads and the nachos and ask about the lobster dishes, fresh fish, and various other specials of the day. Sometimes just the dinner menu is offered at lunch and these portions are large, but two people can share an order. Check out the daily margarita specials and the tequila tasting the third Wednesday evening of every month. *Closed Mon. 340.693.8400. Just south of Mongoose Junction. LD $-$$*

PANINI BEACH

White latticework marks the entrance to this very casual Italian restaurant. Although there are a few inside tables, most everyone surely will want to dine outside, with the beach a step away, the waters of Cruz Bay softly lapping, and the twinkling nighttime lights. There's a penne with sausage and mascarpone, capellini with basil and sun-dried tomatoes, and seared tuna encrusted with pepper on a bed of caramelized onions. Pizzas, salads, and panini are offered at lunch. *Closed for lunch Sat., Sun. 340.693.9119. Wharfside Village. LD $$*

PATOIS

The drink names—Neon Voodoo, Suzanne-Gria, and N'awlins Margarita—set the scene for this Cajun-themed casual eatery. Order a side of jalapeno cornbread while you peruse the menu. Why not begin with a bowl of gumbo or Redneck Scampi or perhaps the cabbage salad? Then try the Kitchen Sink Jambalaya or the Catfish Two Ways (half blackened, half fried), or the barbecued shrimp with red beans and rice. *Closed Sun. 340.715.4270. Across from First Bank. D $$*

WOODY'S SEAFOOD SALOON

Locals and vacationers fill this joint up inside and out every afternoon for happy hour and then come back for burgers, fries, fritters, and icy-cold beers and drinks all night long (the kitchen doesn't close until 1 a.m). *340.779.4625. Across from First Bank. LD $*

117

CRUZ BAY BARS AND ENTERTAINMENT

BANANA DECK

There's a long bar with a TV at the top level of this casual eatery. *340.693.5055. Across from south end of Wharfside Village.*

CHLOE & BERNARD'S

For a quiet and sophisticated bar and lounge head to the atrium level of the Westin St. John. You'll find wines and champagnes by the glass and elegant entertainment three nights a week from 7 p.m. to 10 p.m. (It's usually piano and vocalist Mondays and Wednesdays, and guitar and vocalist Fridays.) *340.714.6075. Five minutes west of Cruz Bay.*

DOCKSIDE PUB

People just off the ferry generally head straight here for an icy-cold beer before they catch a cab, rent a car, or decide what they are going to do next. *340.693.8855. Just to the right as you come off the ferry dock.*

DUFFY'S LOVE SHACK

This is the sister joint to the longtime St. Thomas favorite of the same name and it sports the same thatched-roof bar and is the place to come for a huge array of tropical drinks, frozen drinks, and flaming drinks. They serve food, too. *340.776.6065. Behind Sparky's.*

GECKO GAZEBO & SUN DOG CAFE

Pause in between shops at this charming, little outdoor bar. Check out the daily drink specials and the menu, which includes pizzas, salads, and sandwiches. *340.693.8340. Mongoose Junction.*

LIME INN

There's a bar at the entrance to the restaurant and, tucked way back in the left corner of this popular restaurant is a small, but equally popular bar. *Closed Sun. 340.776.6425. Lemon Tree Mall.*

MARGARITA PHIL'S

When you're in the mood for margaritas, head directly here for one of their daily margarita specials. Check out the tequila tasting the third Wednesday of every month. *Closed Mon. 340.693.8400. Just south of Mongoose Junction.*

PARADISO

The wood glistens at the long and handsome bar in this upscale restaurant. *Closed Sun. 340.693.8899. Mongoose Junction.*

RUMBALAYA
The bar and tables overlook the water at this hot spot just at the end of the ferry dock. Count on evening entertainment Thursday through Saturday (nightly on season). *Closed Sun. 340.714.6169. Wharfside Village.*

STONE TERRACE
The al fresco bar is designed in a broad "U" and locals and visitors belly-up to trade tales of their day's adventures. You can also dine at the bar and drink and/or dine at the little tables in the bar area. *Closed Mon. 340.693.9370. Across from the south end of Wharfside Village.*

WOODY'S SEAFOOD SALOON
Day and night this place is packed and you can eat until 1 a.m. *340.779.4625. Across from First Bank.*

ZOZO'S
People flock to the open-air, third-floor bar here at the end of the day to watch the extraordinary Caribbean sunsets. During certain times of the year, the sun sets in the water instead of behind another island and you can actually catch the famous green flash. *340.693.9200. Gallow's Point.*

CORAL BAY RESTAURANTS & BARS
ISLAND BLUES
This casual waterfront eatery is Coral Bay's best. Tables overlook the water on a little gravel terrace, and more tables are upstairs in the bar area. The menu is varied and the food is superb. Try the meatloaf or a cheeseburger or portobello with goat cheese and red peppers. But before you order check out the blackboard for the outstanding specials of the day, which will include at least two quesadilla choices plus a soup and a sandwich. The quesadilla might be a perfect blend of barbecued beef, cheddar cheese, and onions. The sandwich might be a blackened tuna with wasabi mayonnaise. There's a popular happy hour and frequent evening entertainment. *340.693.5630.* LD $

SHIPWRECK LANDING
Dine casually al fresco on burgers, Caesar salad, Greek salad, fish 'n' chips, taco salad, pasta specials here. *Bands Wed.-Thurs. eves. 340.693.5640.* LD $

SKINNY LEGS BAR AND RESTAURANT
Come to this casual, popular spot for a grilled portobella mushroom sandwich, or a turkey and swiss cheese sandwich, or great chili dogs, burgers, and grilled fish. Friday nights, there's often a band. *340.779.4982.* LD $

A FEW FACTS ABOUT ST. JOHN

St. John is about the size of Manhattan.

Over two-thirds of the island is a National Park.

All beaches on St. John are open to the public.

St. John is about nine miles long and just under 1300 feet above sea level at its highest point, which is Bordeaux Mountain.

St. John is about the same distance from St. Thomas as it is from Tortola or Norman Island in the British Virgins.

It was first inhabited by Arawak Indians moving up from South America.

And "discovered" by Columbus on his second voyage in 1493.

Although it sometimes seems like too many cars on the island now, there weren't any cars on the island at all until the 1950's.

St. John is home to about 4,200 residents and is a vacationing destination for many, many more.

CHAPTER 10

GREAT ST. JOHN SHOPPING, OUTDOOR ACTIVITIES

"So I said to her,
'We're on vacation,
let's enjoy some outdoor activities.'
'Shopping is an outdoor activity,'
she replied."

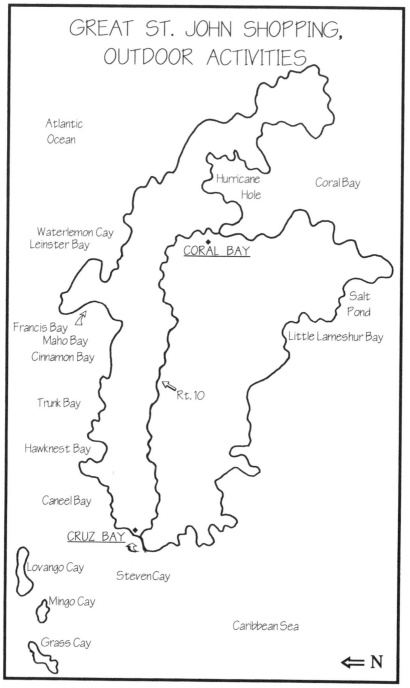

GREAT ST. JOHN SHOPPING, OUTDOOR ACTIVITIES

Atlantic Ocean

Hurricane Hole

Coral Bay

Waterlemon Cay
Leinster Bay

CORAL BAY

Salt Pond

Francis Bay
Maho Bay
Cinnamon Bay

Little Lameshur Bay

Rt. 10

Trunk Bay

Hawknest Bay

Caneel Bay

CRUZ BAY

Lovango Cay

Steven Cay

Mingo Cay

Caribbean Sea

Grass Cay

N

GREAT ST. JOHN SHOPPING

Shopping on St. John is a pleasure. It's almost entirely located in downtown Cruz Bay and there are many superb, one-of-a-kind places. Also, none get ridiculously crowded the way stores can in Charlotte Amalie on St. Thomas. Shops are clustered in three areas. Mongoose Junction is a five-minute walk north of the ferry dock, and its beautiful stonework walls and arches make it one of the prettiest shopping areas anywhere. Wharfside Village is right on the water, south of the ferry dock. In between, "in the middle of town," are still more stores. You can cover all of Cruz Bay on foot in about an hour or half a day, depending on what kind of shopper you are. And remember, just about anything you find can be shipped directly to your home.

MONGOOSE JUNCTION

BAMBOULA

Handsome armoires and cabinets show off a mix of clothing, textiles, Caribbean jewelry, and pottery. You'll find comfy, stylish island clothing for women—long, loose cotton or rayon dresses, slinky camisoles, even shoes; island shirts, pants, and shorts for men; and, further on into the store, bedspreads, cosmetics, cotton throws, and woven baskets. *340.693.8699.*

BEST OF BOTH WORLDS

Don't miss this outstanding gallery, which is a showcase of creativity. Look for appealing metal and wire sculptures, fine oil and watercolor paintings, silver and gold jewelry, some really whimsical creations, superbly restful waterfalls, stunning clocks, colorful frogs. Be sure to look up to catch all the great things hanging from the ceiling, and check out the upstairs, where there's more of everything. Any item here can be shipped anywhere. *340.693.7005.*

BIG PLANET

Get ready for anything you might want to do outdoors with a stop in this multi-level store, which features swimwear, active wear, sundresses, sunglasses, footwear, backpacks, luggage, and accessories from Patagonia, Teva, Jams World, Timberland, and Birkenstock for the whole family. *340.776.6638.*

BOUGAINVILLEA

Come here for a huge selection of upscale, stylish men's and women's clothing (shirts, pants, shoes, sweaters, purses, hats, bags) including Tommy Bahama and Axis, and a potpourri of appealing gift items. A smaller sister store is located at the Westin St. John. *340.693.7190.*

123

CANVAS FACTORY
Practical, durable canvas is the specialty here, fashioned into colorful briefcases, purses, and satchels in all sizes. You'll also find a superb collection of hats. *340.776.6196.*

CARAVAN GALLERY
A curving staircase leads upstairs to this display of unusual items from around the world. Look for dancing frogs, delicate silver and gold chains, exotic masks, sculptures and figurines, and other collectibles. *340.779.4566.*

CLOTHING STUDIO
Watch artists hand-paint everything from bathing suits to hats, T-shirts, sundresses, and cover-ups at this popular shop. *340.776.6585.*

FABRIC MILL
Come here for comfortable, casual island wear: linen and cotton pants, dresses, skirts, and tops in pastels and prints (including a lovely hand-painted white-on-white linen pants and top), plus sarongs, purses, tote bags, books, and unique gift items. Upstairs, shelves are filled with bedspreads, pillows, and table linens—all in beautiful colors and designs. *340.776.6194.*

R&I PATTON GOLDSMITHING
Owners Rudy and Irene Patton design the highly original gold and silver jewelry you'll see at this superb jewelry store. Look for delicate seahorse earrings, a trio of dancing lizards on a pin, a charm bracelet of different tropical fish, a sea turtle pendant, plus unique chains and rings. Tahitian pearls, gemstones, and opal inlay are also specialties. *340.776.6548.*

ST. JOHN EDITIONS
Upscale suburban and resort clothes are featured in this cozy store, plus cocktail dresses, shoes, and lacy lingerie. *Set back against a hill just south of Mongoose Junction, heading to town. 340.693.8444.*

WHARFSIDE VILLAGE
CRUZ BAY CLOTHING COMPANY
Racks are jam-packed with an impressive array of bathing suits, cover-ups, and T-shirts, plus Fresh Produce clothing and Jimmy Buffet shirts. *340.693.8686.*

EVERY TING
Watercolors, candles, greeting cards, island books, unique Caribbean gift items, plus internet and e-mail access and a cappuccino bar make this a one-stop shopping pleasure. *Just south of Wharfside Village. 340.693.5820.*

FREEBIRD

This little shop is a good spot to pick up incense sticks, toe rings, ear swords and shackles, and New Age reading material. They also sell sterling silver and gold jewelry and the pale blue larimar stone. *340.693.8625.*

KHARMA

Don't miss this wonderful shop for women, with its appealing, eclectic mix—lacy camisoles, strapless sundresses, slinky island wear, and other clothing by Betsy Johnson, etc., plus delightful purses in many fabrics and designs, hats, sarongs, watercolors, jewelry, and more. *340.714.7263.*

PUSSER'S LTD.

Come here for Pusser's famous rum; nautical memorabilia; books about the Caribbean; plus Pusser's comfortable, casual clothing—pants, sweaters, shirts, shorts, shirts, bathing suits—for the whole family. *340.693.8489.*

ST. JOHN SPICE

The enticing aromas will draw you into this emporium of spices, coffees, teas, hot sauces, jellies, jams, and more. *340.693.7046.*

MIDDLE OF TOWN

PINK PAPAYA

Pink is just the beginning at this colorful shop, which features the work of St. John artist M. Lisa Etre! Just about everything here is in bright pastel solids and prints: oversize pillows, table linens, hand-painted dinnerware, ceramic bowls, coffee cups, stained glass ornaments, wacky sculptures, and even the colorful books and the Caribbean art displayed on the walls. *340.693.8535.*

SILVERLINING

This tiny shop features lovely, handcrafted jewelry—bracelets, earrings, rings—plus appealing, interesting pottery. *340.693.7766.*

NOW & ZEN

Look for exotic incense, silky tops and pants, purses, creams, and other treasures from the Far East. *340.714.1088.*

CANEEL BAY RESORT SHOP

Definitely worth a stop is this terrific shop, stocked with resortwear for men and women, superb women's swimwear, jewelry, pottery, current paperbacks, books on the islands, plus colorful T-shirts, sweatshirts, glassware, and beach towels emblazoned with the famous Caneel petroglyph logo. *340.776.6111.*

OUTDOOR ACTIVITIES

St. John is an outdoor paradise, above the water and below. There are terrific hiking and horseback riding trails, stunning beaches, calm swimming waters, and spectacular snorkeling. Luckily, much of the island is protected by the U.S. National Park Service. The Virgin Islands National Park includes just over half of St. John plus almost all of the north shore beaches, some south shore beaches, and the waters around these beaches. Watersports come first in this chapter, followed by landsports.

BEACHES AND SNORKELING

Check the map at the beginning of this chapter for beach locations.

HAWKSNEST BAY

The reefs are close to shore at this narrow beach which gets crowded because it's so close to Cruz Bay. You can climb over the rocks at the west end of this beach to a small, more private beach. **Snorkeling:** Three reefs run out from the beach. Look for squid, damselfish, all kinds of angelfish, flatworms, and anemones. Snorkeling won't be good during north swells. *North shore.*

TRUNK BAY

Trunk Bay is a calm bay bordered by a gorgeous sweep of white sand fringed with sea grape and palm trees. This beach makes every list of the world's most beautiful beaches, so, unfortunately, it's no secret. Cruise ships send taxi-loads of passengers here. Trunk is still worth a visit, but to avoid the crowds come in the early morning or late afternoon. There's a $4 entrance fee from 7:30 a.m. to 4:30 p.m. for those 16 and older. **Snorkeling:** Look for the 225-foot, underwater, marked snorkel trail you can follow, with helpful signs identifying what you see. Trunk Bay is an excellent place to spot sea turtles and rays. Reefs full of fish are at both ends of the beach. Look for parrot fish, snappers, tang, and trunkfish and for caves and ledges at the western reef. *Snorkel trail, picnic area, snack bar, souvenir shop, snorkel rentals. North shore.*

CINNAMON BAY

At well over half a mile, this is the island's longest beach. It can be windy here and is a good windsurfing spot. **Snorkeling:** It's especially good along the rocky east end. *Watersports center with snorkel and windsurfer rentals, snorkeling and scuba diving lessons and excursions, campground, restaurant, store. North shore.*

MAHO BAY
Beginning swimmers like the exceptionally calm waters and the fact that the water is so shallow for a long way out. There's no sign for this beach but you can see it from the road and you can park right at the edge of the beach. **Snorkeling:** It's a good place to catch sight of rays and turtles. *North shore.*

FRANCIS BAY
A long, narrow beach runs along this well-protected bay and the water is very calm. **Snorkeling:** This is a terrific snorkeling stop. Look for coral at the western edge, sea turtles out in the bay, octopus at the east end. You'll also see parrot fish, blue tang, and damselfish. *North shore.*

LEINSTER BAY/WATERLEMON CAY
The beach here is tiny and a bit rocky but Waterlemon Cay, which is at the eastern edge of big and beautiful Leinster Bay, is an outstanding snorkel spot. Beware of currents. **Snorkeling:** Spot sea turtles, stingrays, octopus, peacock flounder, sponges, seastars (starfish), and schools of parrot fish. *North shore.*

SALTPOND BAY
You'll find fewer people at this wide beach than at many of the north shore beaches. **Snorkeling:** Look in the rocky areas for octopus and moray eels. This is also a good place to see angelfish, grunts, snappers, turtles, conch, and stingrays. *South shore.*

LITTLE LAMESHUR BAY
Expect to find few people at this remote beach. The drive is a bit rough but you end up right at the beach. **Snorkeling:** You'll see all kinds of fish among the eastern rocks and along the western shoreline. This is also a good place to catch a look at sea turtles and rays. *South shore.*

BOATING

DAY SAILS
You'll find a number of charter boats in Cruz Bay that will take you out for a half- or full-day sail or even a sunset sail.

Cruz Bay Watersports offers two great day sail adventures. There's a day sail to Virgin Gorda's Baths on the 60' *Island Time* every Monday, Wednesday, and Friday. This trip includes a continental breakfast, lunch, snorkel gear, and an open bar. There's also a day trip to Jost Van Dyke on the 40' powerboat *Blast* every Tuesday, Thursday, and Saturday. This trip includes snorkeling, lunch at Foxy's, and a stop in White Bay on the way home. *Per person rates: Virgin Gorda Trip $110 plus fee for customs, Jost Van Dyke trip $110 including fee for customs. Cruz Bay. 340.776.6234.*

Hurricane Alley features a 51' Hinkley, which takes a maximum of six people. A full-day sail includes a long sail, a buffet lunch at anchor, and an afternoon snorkel. They also offer an hour-and-a-half sunset cruise on the same sailboat and a half-day snorkel trip on a powerboat which stops at two snorkel spots on other islands. *Per person rates: Full day on Hinkley $115; sunset cruise $65 ($350 for a private sunset cruise); powerboat snorkel trip $50. Mongoose Junction. 340.776.6256.*

PARASAILING

Cruz Bay Watersports offers parasailing, an exciting and popular sport, from the Westin dock every hour. The cost is $65 to "fly" and $15 to ride in the boat. *Cruz Bay. 340.776.6234.*

RENTING POWERBOATS

When the water is calm, it can be a wonderful adventure to rent your own little powerboat and head out to an uninhabited island for the day. You can easily go to Grass, Mingo, or Lovango Cay, where there are little beaches, or to Whistling Cay, where there is the ruin of a house along a beach. You can even go to the British Virgin Islands (see page 94).

Ocean Runner Powerboat Rentals rents 22', 25', and 28' powerboats, each with a bimini, VHS radio, and cooler. You can hire a captain if you want, and rent snorkel and fishing gear. *$275-$375 per day (less off-season). Wharfside Village, Cruz Bay. 340.693.8809.*

Nauti Nymph rents 25', 29', and 31' power boats with bimini, VHS, cooler, and fresh water shower. You may captain yourself or hire a captain and, of course, rent snorkel gear. *$315-$425 (less off-season). Westin dock. 340.775.5066 or 800.734.7345.*

SEA KAYAKING

The waters around St. John offer great sea kayaking opportunities. There are cays to explore, and snorkeling spots to visit.

Arawak Expeditions rents kayaks and also has several guided excursions. Three-hour trips leave at 9 a.m. and 2 p.m. for a nearby cay and some snorkeling. Full-day trips depart at 10 a.m. for several uninhabited cays and snorkeling. They also have overnight and multi-day camping trips. *$50 half-day, $90 full-day. Cruz Bay. 340.693.8312.*

WAVERUNNERS

The versatile **Cruz Bay Watersports** also offers guided waverunner tours in and around Pillsbury Sound. A single person waverunner is $75 and a two-person is $90. *Cruz Bay. 340.776.6234.*

DIVING

DIVING TRIPS

The underwater geography around St. John is shallow but there are still great 30' to 50' dives.

Cruz Bay Watersports takes certified divers out every morning for a two-tank dive. Pickup is 8:15 a.m. at the Westin Dock. You're in the water a few minutes later. The daily afternoon trip (1:15 p.m. at the Westin Dock) is a one-tank dive but they also take snorkelers and give scuba lessons. *Morning $85; afternoon $65; snorkelers $55; non-certified divers $95. Cruz Bay. 340.776.6234.*

SNORKELING HINTS

❑When it is sunny, you'll see more and it will be clearer if you snorkel between 8 a.m. to 10 a.m.

❑Protect the reefs. Coral is extremely fragile and it grows very slowly. Never touch it, never step on it with your flippers, and never anchor your boat in coral.

❑Watch out for black blobs with spikes nestled in the rocks. These are sea urchins and they sting. The bigger they are, the worse the pain.

❑Parrot fish make their own little sleeping bags each night. If you spot things that look like little plastic sacs, it could be sleeping fish.

❑Speaking of parrot fish, they are big beach builders. They and other reef fish eat algae that grows on coral and inadvertently also take in bits of the coral skeletons, which they later excrete as sand!

❑If you want to dive a bit deeper than you can comfortably snorkel, but don't want tanks on your back, try **Snuba**. The air tank remains on a float above the water and follows you around. *Reservations necessary. Mon.-Sat. 11 a.m. and 1 p.m., Sun. 1 p.m. $57. Trunk Bay. 340.693.8063.*

LANDSPORTS

BIRD-WATCHING

In winter months, bird lovers head to the Francis Bay Trail where they hope to spot a West Indian whistling duck, yellow-billed cuckoo, and some of the other more than 160 species of birds that live in this area.

HIKING

The National Park Service maintains over 20 hiking trails that lead through mountain forests and dry cactus and along old plantation roads to extraordinary beaches, overlooks with breathtaking views of the sea and neighboring islands, and historic sugar plantation ruins. Trails vary greatly in degree of difficulty and length and range from 10 minutes to three hours. Pick up a copy of the Virgin Islands National Park Trail Guide (count on trail times taking a little longer than stated) and be sure to bring plenty of drinking water with you. *National Park Visitor Center, Cruz Bay. 340.776.6201.*

HIKES WITH GUIDES

The National Park Service offers guided hikes down steep Reef Bay Trail, which includes a visit to sugar mill ruins and to ancient petroglyphs, and ends at a beach. Although signs along the way make this an easy trip to do on your own, the guided trip returns via boat while everyone else has a steep, two-mile hike back up the trail! *Call for reservations as soon as you know your vacation plans (hikes fill up fast). Mon., Thurs., Fri. $5 to head of trail, $20 for guided hike, $15 for boat ride back (all rates per person). 340.776.6201.*

HORSEBACK AND DONKEY RIDING

Go horseback or donkey riding along scenic trails up into the mountains or down to the beach. You can even go swimming with your horse! Carolina Corral Trail Rides offers three one-and-a-half-hour rides per day at 10 a.m., 2 p.m., and 5 p.m. *$55 per rider (cash or traveler's check only). 340.693.5778.*

MOUNTAIN BIKE TOURS

Catch stunning scenery, visit beaches and historic ruins, and find splendid photo ops biking around the island. **Arawak Expeditions** offers tours for both the novice and experienced cyclists. *$45 per person half day; $80 per person full day. 340.693.8312.*

TENNIS

Tennis anyone? There are beautiful courts at Caneel Bay and the Westin St. John. If you are staying at either resort, court use is complimentary. If you are staying elsewhere, you may use the courts for a fee. Call and ask for the Tennis Shop. *Caneel Bay 340.776.6111; Westin St. John 340.693.8000.*

SECTION III

WATER ISLAND & HASSEL ISLAND

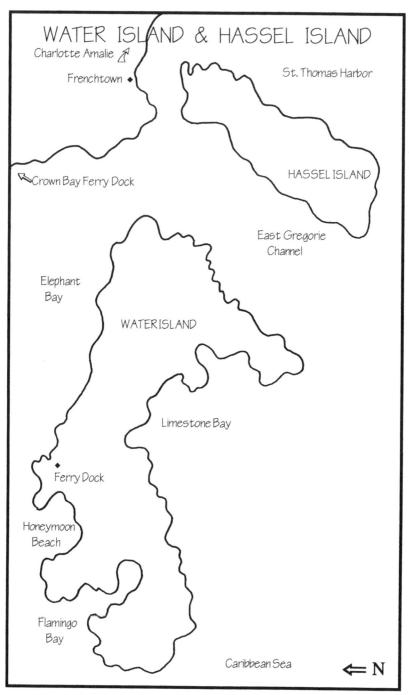

WATER ISLAND & HASSEL ISLAND

Charlotte Amalie

Frenchtown

St. Thomas Harbor

HASSEL ISLAND

Crown Bay Ferry Dock

East Gregorie
Channel

Elephant
Bay

WATER ISLAND

Limestone Bay

Ferry Dock

Honeymoon
Beach

Flamingo
Bay

Caribbean Sea

N

WATER ISLAND

Less than a half-mile off the south shore of St. Thomas lies Water Island, the fourth largest U.S. Virgin Island. Visiting Water Island is a great daytime adventure and vacationing on the island can be a great way to enjoy splendid isolation yet be just 10 minutes by boat from sophisticated St. Thomas dining and shopping.

Like its sister U.S. Virgin Islands, Water Island is quite hilly and has a curvaceous shoreline. It's also quite small at just under 492 acres. The island is about two miles long and its width varies from about one-third of a mile to about 400 yards. The highest point is 294' and there are about 150 residents. Water Island has a pretty little curve of a beach known as Honeymoon Beach and another beach quite good for snorkeling. There are private residences, some rental properties, and an occasional car, but there is not one single store on the island, and the only "restaurant" is a beach affair open on weekends.

A DAYTIME BEACH ADVENTURE

For a great daytime beach adventure, head over to Crown Bay Marina, which is just west of Charlotte Amalie, and catch the ferry to Water Island. It runs quite often and it's easy to go for a full day or just the morning or afternoon. (*See page 135 for the complete schedule*). The fare is $5 per person one-way.

You'll see the little open-air boat alongside the dock in front of Tickles Restaurant and Bar at Crown Bay Marina. Just hop on and wait. The pilot will show up soon enough (he's usually off getting supplies for the island). The trip takes five minutes. There are no facilities here so you'll need to bring everything you might want to have with you—towels, sunscreen, a cooler with water and sodas, and perhaps lunch. Or have lunch at Tickles (*see description page 49*) before or after your trip. Or, if you come on Saturday or Sunday, you can dine at the informal beach grill on Honeymoon Beach. Heidi usually starts cooking around noon and prepares burgers, Italian sausages, grilled chicken, and Caesar salads, and sells sodas and beers. Many Saturday nights she cooks up several pasta dishes and grills steaks and serves dinner at candlelit picnic tables on the beach from 7 p.m. to 9 p.m.

Water Island has a good swimming beach and a good snorkeling beach. Honeymoon Beach is a gentle curve of white sand and the water is very calm. It's over a steep rise but easily walkable from the dock in about 15 minutes.

133

Just follow the road up and down. This is a great beach for sunning and relaxing. (Bear in mind that weekdays the KonTiki Party Boat brings boisterous revelers to this beach for a few hours in the early afternoon). On the other side of the island is coral Limestone Beach, which is rocky on the feet but has good snorkeling. This beach is a bit of a haul (a very long hike up and down) but you can sometimes find a ride. You can also hike to see the remnants of an old fort up on the hill. The views are terrific. Ask someone at the dock for directions to the fort. If you plan to hike around, bring plenty of drinking water.

GETTING AWAY FROM IT ALL
FOR A WEEK, OR EVEN A MONTH

Staying on Water Island is a great way to enjoy delightful isolation without being truly isolated. Despite the fact that you are on an island with only 150 other people and no stores or restaurants you are not "in the middle of nowhere." You can pretend to be a zillion miles from anything, but when you need fresh garlic, or want to shop, or crave a meal in a fancy restaurant you can hop on the ferry for a five-minute boat ride to St. Thomas. Once there, dine at the casual restaurant right at the ferry dock (where you can have breakfast, lunch, or dinner) or take a five-minute cab ride to the great restaurants in Frenchtown and Charlotte Amalie.

When you stay on Water Island, the pleasures are of the simple kind. There's not much to do except relax, think, read, or take in the views. Head down to Honeymoon Beach for a peaceful swim or over to Limestone Beach for a good snorkel. Or spend time in the kitchen cooking a dinner to enjoy under the stars. By the way, stargazing is outstanding here. And when you need more supplies, what an adventure to take a ferry over for groceries and whatever else you need.

WATERFRONT COTTAGE

A perfect Water Island choice is the Waterfront Cottage on Providence Point, part of a family-owned hilltop compound of several houses. Set 70' above the water's edge, this spacious two-bedroom cottage has a full kitchen and looks out to stunning sky and ocean views. The ferry dock and Honeymoon Beach are short walks away. Cottage renters share a stunning disappearing-edge pool (the largest pool on the island) with the owners (and children), who live in a house across the point, and with whoever might be renting the two smaller two-bedroom houses on the property. Buildings are discretely placed. Both the cottage and smaller houses have satellite TV and internet connections.

1 cottage, 2 smaller houses. Bi-weekly maid service. Weekly rates Thanksgiving-Easter: Cottage $1,500 ($1,200 off-season); villa apartments $1,200 ($1,000 off-season). Tel: 340.774.2635. Fax: 340.776.1316. www.water-island.com

St. Thomas-Water Island Ferry Schedule
Monday-Saturday

From St. Thomas	From Water Island
6:30 a.m.	6:45 a.m.
7:15 a.m.	7:30 a.m.
8:00 a.m.	10:45 a.m.
10:30 a.m.	12:15 (M,W,F,Sat.)
12 noon (M,W,F,Sat.)	2:15 p.m.
2:00 p.m.	4:30 p.m.
4:15 p.m.	5:30 p.m.
5:15 p.m.	6:10 p.m.
6:00 p.m.	

NIGHT RUNS (Mon., Wed., Fri., Sat.)

9:00 p.m.	9:15 p.m.

Sunday (and Holidays)

8:00 a.m.	8:15 a.m.
12:00 p.m.	12:15 p.m.
5:00 p.m.	5:15 p.m.

This schedule is subject to change. Call 340.690.4159 or 340.690.4446 or check the schedule at the dock in front of Tickles. Per person fare is $5 one-way, $9 round-trip, more for night runs. Inquire about late night and off-schedule runs which are available for a fee.

HASSEL ISLAND

It can be a bit of a hassle getting to Hassel Island but if you are the adventurous type, you might find it a lot of fun.

This is the island that sits right in the middle of St. Thomas harbor. Although there are a few private residences, most of the 135-acre island is part of the Virgin Islands National Park. Trails have not been maintained but if you want a bit of a rugged hike, it is possible to follow them. The National Register of Historic Places lists four spots on this island, including an old coal mining station and shipyard. These are unrestored and pretty much in ruin at the moment. Occasionally there are guided hikes. *Call 340.775.6238 or 340.776.6201, ext. 252 for information.* So how do you get here? Try calling the **Water Island Ferry** (*340.690.4159 or 340.690.4446*). Sometimes they will drop you off and pick you up and, if not, they can put you in touch with someone who can.

PRACTICAL INFORMATION
BANKING AND ATMS

On St. Thomas, First Bank has four branches with ATMs, including one on the Waterfront in Charlotte Amalie and one at Port of Sale at Havensight. First Bank also has a branch and ATM in Cruz Bay on St. John. The Westin St. John has an ATM in their lobby. ATM machines in the islands are sometimes less reliable than stateside ATMs, so don't always count on getting cash from them.

CAR RENTALS

Virtually all car rental agencies will pick you up at your resort and some resorts have rental agencies right on the premises. Cars run about $50 a day. On both St. Thomas and St. John, on-season, it is best to make your reservations well ahead of time to be sure of getting a car. Driving is on the left.

CAR RENTALS ON ST. THOMAS: If you are staying at a full-service resort, you may not want to rent a car. The St. Thomas road system is hilly and trafficky and it is easy to get lost. Taxis are available everywhere to take you to and from restaurants, beaches, or even on a tour around the island (*see Taxis page 139 and pages 42-43*). If you do decide to rent a car for a day of exploring or for your entire visit, try **Avis** (*800.331.1084, 340.774.1468*) which has locations at the airport, the Renaissance, and Marriott Frenchmans Reef; **Budget** (*800.626.4516, 340.776.5774*) which has locations at the airport, Havensight, and Sapphire Beach; **Hertz** (*800.654.3131, 340.774.0841*) which has an airport location; or **Dependable Car** (*800.522.3076 or 340.774.2253*), a local and highly reliable rental agency three minutes from the airport.

CAR RENTALS ON ST. JOHN: Many visitors to St. John will want to rent a car (usually a jeep), if not for their whole stay, at least for a day. It is fun to spend time on St. John visiting one beach after another and the main roads, although quite hilly, are well-paved and clearly marked (beware that side roads are a completely different story—if you venture off the beaten track, be prepared for roads that turn into rocky messes leading to nowhere). Call **Hertz** (*800.654.3131, 340.693.7580*), **O'Conner Car Rental** (*340.776.6343*), or **Lionel Jeep Rental** (*340.693.8764*), a local company with excellent service. *Note: If you are staying on one of the more remote locations on St. John, you will want to pick up your car in Cruz Bay before you check in.*

CRIME

On St. Thomas, act carefully, the same way you would in any city. Watch for pickpockets in Charlotte Amalie, especially when it is crowded. Don't walk at night; instead, drive or take cabs. On St. John, it is safe to walk around Cruz Bay at night. On both islands, don't leave valuables visible in your car, even if it is locked, and don't leave your wallet or jewelry lying about in your hotel room (if there is a safe in your hotel room, use it).

CURRENCY, CREDIT CARDS, AND TIPPING
The currency is the U.S. dollar. Most places take credit cards but you may encounter an occasional establishment that takes only cash or traveler's checks, so bring some along. Also, some establishments refuse to take American Express so be sure to bring a MasterCard or Visa. There is no sales tax but there is an 8% hotel tax and some hotels add a 10% (or more) service charge. Restaurants vary, and usually no service is added, so tip as you would in the states (15%-20%); if 10% service is added, then make up the difference to get to 15%-20%; if 15% service is added, only add more if you want to. Most restaurants clearly state on the menu and the bill whether or not they include a service charge. If you are at all unsure, just ask.

CUSTOMS AND DUTY-FREE SHOPPING
Each U.S. visitor, including children, can return with (or mail) $1,200 worth of duty-free imported goods from the U.S. Virgin Islands every 30 days. U.S. residents 21 years of age or over may return with 4 litres of liquor duty-free (5 litres if one is locally produced, like Virgin Islands rum). You clear customs in St. Thomas and, if you are flying via San Juan, occasionally also San Juan.

DOCUMENTS
Although no identification is necessary to enter the USVI, **you will need a picture identification plus proof of citizenship**, such as a birth certificate or passport, **to depart the USVI. If you have a current passport, bring it. You will find that having a current passport makes the process of clearing customs and immigration much smoother and less problematic.** Also, once you see how close the British Virgin Islands are, you'll probably want to head there for a day and you MUST have a valid passport to enter the BVI.

DRIVING
First of all, it's on the left. Secondly, these are extremely hilly islands and the roads are steep and curvy. Be very careful when it rains. Islanders drive fast and tailgate. Try to ignore the tailgating or pull over and let them pass. Main roads are well-paved but side roads aren't. This is particularly true on St. John.

GETTING TO AND FROM ST. THOMAS AND ST. JOHN
GETTING TO AND FROM ST. THOMAS: You can fly to St. Thomas's Cyril E. King airport nonstop from many U.S. cities. **American** (*800.433.7300*) has nonstop service from Miami, New York/JFK, and Boston (seasonally). **Continental** (*800.231.0856*) offers nonstop service from Newark. **Delta** (*800.221.1212*) flies nonstop from Atlanta. **United** (*800.864.8331*) has Saturday nonstop service from Washington, D.C. and Chicago. **U.S. Airways** (*800.622.1015*) offers nonstop service from Philadelphia and Charlotte. In

137

addition, **American** also flies direct from many U.S. cities to San Juan, and connects these flights with American Eagle flights to St. Thomas. If you are flying via San Juan, bear in mind that in San Juan you should get to your American Eagle gate early, because at the gate you will board a bus and be driven out to your plane. The San Juan connection can be somewhat chaotic and many people who must make a connnection prefer to make it in the states (for instance, nonstop to Atlanta or Miami, then nonstop to St. Thomas). If you need a flight from San Juan to St. Thomas, call **American Eagle** (*800.433.7300*), **Cape Air** (*800.352.0714*), or **LIAT** (*340.774.2313*).

GETTING TO AND FROM ST. JOHN: St. John has no airport and people fly to St. Thomas and then take a ferry to St. John. Ferries run regularly from both Charlotte Amalie and Red Hook on St. Thomas (*see ferry schedule, page 140*) to Cruz Bay on St. John. If you are staying at Caneel Bay or the Westin St. John, you can check in at their airport check-in locations (just beyond the baggage carriage), and then be taken to their private ferries which go directly to the resort. If several of you are traveling together to St. John, you may prefer to travel by private warer taxi (*call **Dohm Water Taxi**, 340.775.6501*).

LODGING

Don't assume that even the fanciest lodging on St. Thomas and St. John will equal the service, cuisine, and amenities one can expect to find in a full-service, luxury stateside resort. Remember, you are in the Caribbean. So relax, slow down, and enjoy the view.

PUBLIC HOLIDAYS

The USVI celebrate all major U.S. holidays. Banks and virtually all shops will be closed on these days. Carnival is a two-week festival. On St. Thomas, it is tied into Easter. On St. John it ends on the Fourth of July.

SPECIAL NEEDS

Accessible Adventures (*866.282.7223, www.accessvi.com*) offers tours for guests that have mobility restrictions. On both St. Thomas and St. John these tours focus on historical sites and beautiful scenery. On St. John the **St. John Community Foundation** (*340.693.7600*) offers tours aboard an accessible van. At Trunk Bay there is **De-Bug**, an all-terrain vehicle that makes the trip from the parking lot to the water's edge much easier for visitors with mobility challenges. Call the Virgin Islands National Park Service (*340.776.6201*) for information. **DIAL-A-RIDE** (*340.776.1277*) offers transportation services and tours on St. Thomas for persons with disabilities. Persons with disabilities who wish to go diving can call **Aqua Center** (*340.775.6285*) or the **Admiralty Dive Center** (*340.777.9802*) on St. Thomas. For the most current list of ADA-compliant resorts and hotels, call the USVI Visitors' Bureau (*800.372.8784*) and ask for the most recent edition of the U.S. Virgin Islands Rates brochure.

TAXIS AND BUSES

For information on taxis and how they operate, see pages 42-43. If you want to call a taxi on St. Thomas, good taxis include **EverReady Taxi Service** (*340.473.7445*), **Sunshine Taxi** (*340.775.1145*), and **Asner Bellevue** (*340.776.0676 or 340.643.7849*). VITRAN buses also cover popular routes on both St. Thomas and St. John.

TELEPHONING AND CELL PHONES AND E-MAIL

The area code for the USVI is 340. When you are calling within the USVI, use the seven-digit number without the area code, even if you are calling from one U.S. Virgin Island to another. Many locals (boat trips, fishing trips, taxi drivers) have cell phones and, sometimes when you dial these numbers you will get an "out of range" recording even when the person is not out of range. Just try the number again. Your stateside cell phone may or may not work in the USVI. Call your provider and ask. If it is supposed to work and you find you are having trouble getting good reception in these islands, go into your settings if you can, until you find protocol stack, and try switching your phone to "TDMA preferred" rather than "GSM preferred." If you can bear it, try turning your phone off. If you came to the islands to really "get away from it all" then why not give it a try. For e-mail and the internet see page 93.

TIME

It's Atlantic Standard Time, which is one hour ahead of Eastern Standard Time. However, the USVI does not switch to Daylight Savings Time and during these months the USVI are on the same time as the U.S. eastern time zone.

WEATHER

People often think that the further south one goes, the hotter it gets. Not true! The USVI temperatures hover around 75 degrees in the winter, 85 degrees in the summer and the trade winds almost always blow. New York City can be much hotter in August than the USVI!

WEB SITES: For info on St. John and St. Thomas, go to www.usvitourism.com

WHAT TO BRING

Sunscreen (the USVI are only 18 degrees from the equator and the sun is strong all year long), bug repellant, casual clothes. In the evening at the nicer restaurants on St. Thomas, casual elegant resortwear is appropriate, including long pants and collared shirts for men. St. John is more relaxed, although Caneel Bay and the Westin St. John both require collared shirts and long pants for their fancy restaurants. Bring sturdy shoes if you want to hike and perhaps a light sweater as evenings can be cool any time of year.

FERRY SCHEDULES

BETWEEN CHARLOTTE AMALIE, ST. THOMAS AND CRUZ BAY, ST. JOHN

The Charlotte Amalie ferry dock for this ferry is right at Waterfront Highway, across the road and a bit west of Hibiscus Alley. The ferry ride takes about 45 minutes and the one-way fare is $7. Going to St. John they collect the money on the boat, but from St. John you need to buy a ticket at the booth. Call Transportation Services (*340.776.6412*).

From Charlotte Amalie	From Cruz Bay
9:00 a.m.	7:15 a.m.
11:00 a.m.	9:15 a.m.
1:00 p.m.	11:15 p.m.
3:00 p.m.	1:15 p.m.
4:00 p.m.	2:15 p.m.
5:30 p.m.	3:45 p.m.

BETWEEN RED HOOK, ST. THOMAS AND CRUZ BAY, ST. JOHN

The ferry ride takes about 15 to 20 minutes and the one-way fare is $3 for adults, $1 for children under 12. There is a ticket booth at both docks. Call Transportation Services (*340.776.6282*) or Varlak Ventures (*340.776.6412*) for additional information.

From Red Hook	From Cruz Bay
6:30 a.m.	on the hour
7:30 a.m	6 a.m.-11 p.m
on the hour 8 a.m.-midnight	

BETWEEN CHARLOTTE AMALIE AND MARRIOTT FRENCHMAN'S REEF

A cute little ferry runs between the resort and town, and you can take it from town to the resort to dine or swim at Morningstar Beach. The one-way fare is $5 and it leaves from Waterfront Highway, right across from Rolex.

From Charlotte Amalie

Mon.-Sat. every hour on the hour, 9:00 a.m.-5:00 p.m.
Sun. every hour on the half hour, 9:30 a.m.-4:30 p.m.

From Marriott Frenchman's Reef

Mon.-Sat. every hour on the half hour, 8:30 a.m.-4:30 p.m.
Sun. every hour on the hour, 9:00 a.m.-4:00 p.m.

INDEX

**KEY TO RESTAURANT
SYMBOLS**

**"B" and "L" and "D" appear
at the end of restaurant
descriptions and indicate
whether the establishment
is open for breakfast, lunch,
and/or dinner.**

**$ = INEXPENSIVE
$$ = MODERATE
$$$ = EXPENSIVE**

ABOUT THE AUTHORS

Since escaping from corporate life in Manhattan, husband and wife team Pam Acheson and Dick Myers have spent the last 15 years living in and exploring the Virgin Islands and Florida.

Between them they have authored, written, and contributed to over 60 books, written articles for many national and international magazines, and have been featured guests on dozens of television and radio shows throughout the United States and the Caribbean.

Their extremely knowledgeable, personal, reader-friendly guides to the U.S. Virgin Islands, the British Virgin Islands, and romantic Florida perennially rank among the best sellers for these destinations in the world.

They reside in the Virgin Islands and Florida...and quite enjoy visiting Manhattan.